COUPLE THERAPY

A Complete Guide to Cure and Build a Stronger Relationship

(Develop a Deeper Connection With Your Partner and Improve Intimacy)

Gertrude Savell

Published by Harry Barnes

Gertrude Savell

All Rights Reserved

Couple Therapy: A Complete Guide to Cure and Build a Stronger Relationship (Develop a Deeper Connection With Your Partner and Improve Intimacy)

ISBN 978-1-77485-116-6

All rights reserved. No part of this guide may be reproduced in any form without permission in writing from the publisher except in the case of brief quotations embodied in critical articles or reviews.

Legal & Disclaimer

The information contained in this book is not designed to replace or take the place of any form of medicine or professional medical advice. The information in this book has been provided for educational and entertainment purposes only.

The information contained in this book has been compiled from sources deemed reliable, and it is accurate to the best of the Author's knowledge; however, the Author cannot guarantee its accuracy and validity and cannot be held liable for any errors or omissions. Changes are periodically made to this book. You must consult your doctor or get professional medical advice before using any of the suggested remedies, techniques, or information in this book.

Upon using the information contained in this book, you agree to hold harmless the Author from and against any damages, costs, and expenses, including any legal fees potentially resulting from the application of any of the information provided by this guide. This disclaimer applies to any damages or injury caused by the use and application, whether directly or indirectly, of any advice or information presented, whether for breach of contract, tort, negligence, personal injury, criminal intent, or under any other cause of action.

You agree to accept all risks of using the information presented inside this book. You need to consult a professional medical practitioner in order to ensure you are both able and healthy enough to participate in this program.

Table of Contents

INTRODUCTION 1

CHAPTER 1: COMMUNICATION GUIDELINES 6

CHAPTER 2: THE FOUR STAGES OF LOVE 17

CHAPTER 3: UNDERSTANDING JEALOUSY........................ 32

CHAPTER 4: THE RELATIONSHIP LIFE CYCLE 67

CHAPTER 5: IN A RELATIONSHIP, WHY CONFLICT RESOLUTION SKILLS ARE IMPORTANT 79

CHAPTER 6: ISSUES OF SEX AND AFFECTION.................... 97

CHAPTER 7: TRY THESE NEW TOOLS...WON'T REGRET IT 111

CHAPTER 8: ATTACHMENT THEORY BASICS.................... 123

CHAPTER 9: CREATE OR RE-CREATE INTIMACY -WAYS TO CHARM YOUR PARTNER AND GET THEM TO BE RESPONSIVE TO YOU AND LIKE YOU MORE 130

CHAPTER 10: HANDLING TYPICAL OBSTACLES 143

CHAPTER 11: SIGNIFICANT HABITS OF GOOD RELATIONSHIPS 166

CONCLUSION 176

Introduction

More often than not, the problem I encounter over and over again when dealing with clients is they feel a disconnection with each other, a gap that continues to grow wider and wider in the relationship, tearing couples apart. It has become pretty clear to me a lot of the issues in relationships are centered around a lack of communication, which fosters a feeling of being disconnected. This is why it is important to fix this problem. This is why I felt the burning need to write this book.

As this is a workbook, I will give you and your significant other practical exercises to move through in order to improve the relationship you have, and fix things so it's just like in the good old honeymoon phase — except that you'll be a lot stronger, and wiser now.

Before we jump into the practical exercises though, I will definitely go over a few things that are absolutely essential for every couple in a heterosexual relationship to understand. We're going to touch a bit on the issue of gender equality, and emotional intelligence. I would also like you, dear reader, to understand that each gender has something great to bring to the table. It is my intention to proffer a few solutions to problems which are all too common in most relationships and marriages, so you can begin to work on them as best as you can.

I would like to make it as clear as I can that you can only achieve results from following through with the exercises in this book. Head knowledge is never enough. Also, you cannot talk the talk without walking the walk. You need to have the determination to see your marriage or relationship thrive and survive as it should. That means you're going to have to put in the work.

More often than not, people start out in their relationships pretty well. But then as time goes by, life happens. People get busy, and then you and your loved one pay a lot less attention to each other than you used to. What this naturally implies is there is less nurturing, less care, and less loving going on.

Naturally, this means intimacy between you two plummets, and then you both get irritated with one another more often than not, making it even harder to reconnect and find that spark again. Once it gets to that point, it could feel like it's absolutely impossible to get things back on track. That's why you have this book in your hands: To fix things between you two.

There are a lot of factors which come to play in your relationship, including the way you and your significant other were raised. Your upbringing affects the way you relate to one another, and the way you see the world. While there is nothing you can do about your past, you can at least take charge of the way you respond today.

It is my sincere hope that as you and your spouse work through this book together, you will grow in love and understanding with each other. I intend for you to learn what part you should play in your relationship, as the onus falls on not one, but **both** partners to keep the love thriving.

At present, you may feel like you're stuck in a rut when it comes to your relationship. You might feel like you're incredibly bored, and that anything else would be better than what you have. It might seem to you like the person you fell in love with no longer exists, because it seems they have changed so much.

I want to tell you this: It's not the end of it all. Don't quit on love just yet. I can tell you from personal experience, that there have been couples on the very edge of destruction, who have turned things around for the better, by simply being willing to work together on their relationship, or their marriage. This could be you too. All you need is to be willing and open to change, and to be committed to making time to connect with one another again.

Couples Therapy Workbook will give you the tools you need in order to get the relationship you desire, and even better. In addition to all the ground I have already mentioned we'll cover; we will also address different parts of your relationship each week. All you need is 30 minutes, daily. You can give at least 30 minutes a day where you and the love of your life can connect with each other, and work on building your relationship together as a team.

You should do these exercises as you wind down for the day, at a set time. Make it an appointment, because it is one. It is just as important as a meeting at work; perhaps more so. Also, whenever you think things are starting to go south with you two after doing these exercises, remember, you can always begin anew. Now, let's dive in.

Chapter 1: Communication

Guidelines

In most environments, men and women are brought up differently, which ultimately makes then react differently to forms of communication. For example, women communicate to understand and find equality, while a man will do it as a way to negotiate for power or offer a solution. This simply means that the goal of communication for women will always be different from that of men, and it takes a lot of learning and skill to know how to handle the opposite sex, especially in a relationship setting.

What Makes It Different?

Women: Women are mostly emotional creatures, which is not meant in a negative way. It only means that they attach feelings and emotions to conversations and prefer being listened to more than the problem being solved. They mostly want to be heard and understood, not necessarily sympathized. Women are mostly satisfied with getting information off their chest and knowing that someone understands where they are coming from, which helps them process the situation better.

Men: Men, nevertheless, are more analytical of situations. If a situation is presented to them, they immediately think of fixing it and moving on to the next thing. This means when their partners come to them with frustration, they will listen yes, but then they will start thinking of how to solve the problem to make it better or never recur again. They are mostly solution-oriented and great problem solvers. Unfortunately, this can class with what the woman needs, as they mostly end up feeling like the man does not understand.

Gender Differences in Communication

There are some basic ways of communication that the two genders process differently or do differently. This doesn't make it easy for the two to relate, but when one knows how to go about their way of communicating, then it is easier to nurture great relationships that would last even into marriage. It needs a lot of practice and the different genders, acknowledging that they are wired differently.

Nonverbal Communication

The way women take in nonverbal information is always different from how the men take it. This is why one has to learn and know how to go about it, especially when in an opposite-gender relationship. This is because of the way the different genders are wired to handle it:

Facial expressions: Our faces can give a lot of expression at any given time. However, men use fewer facial expressions compared to women. Whereas women rely more on having facial expressions as a reaction to most things, men will maintain a straight face.

Men generally smile less compared to women, as they conclude that showing too much emotion is not manly. Also, most men avoid having too much show on their faces so that their emotions cannot be easily read. Women are the total opposite, and it is easier to tell what a woman is feeling or thinking by just looking at their facial expressions. When a woman is happy, they will smile a lot, and you can also tell when they are not pleased, as it will easily show on their faces. It is a good and bad thing at the same time because, for men, it helps them cover up some reactions to some situations. For omen, it can be difficult as one can be able to tell upfront what they are thinking.

Touch: When it comes to touch, both genders do it, but they do it differently and to achieve different emotions. A woman will touch or offer a hug, to create a connection or maybe support the other person. However, a man might give a pat on the back or extend greetings, to set a tone of communication or display their dominance. Most men also would not like to build connections with strangers as they are naturally not emotionally attached to things or people.

Men would automatically find it weird being constantly touched by someone, especially of the opposite sex. They take it more personal and find it strange if they do not have a close or personal relationship with the person. It is even worse between men and men, as they see no need for touch. Their emotions are not aroused by random touches.

Women thrive on touch and physical contact. Even among friends, women will touch and feel more connected. In a marriage, the more a woman is touched by their spouse, the more connected and intimate they will feel. They even feel more loved and attracted to their spouse when touched frequently. When a husband doesn't touch their wife often, they will tend to feel unattractive to them, hence disconnect them mentally.

Women, nevertheless, will have a posture depending on the relationship they have with the person. The majority of women fold their arms around their chests, and some cross their legs. It is mostly a sign of seriousness on their end, though at times it comes across as being unapproachable. Most women, when asked, would say it is just a way of them paying more attention to the conversation. They also lean forward more when interested in the person they are talking to or might lean back to show a lack of interest. This is a rare trait to find in men.

Eye contact: this is one of the essential aspects of communication. Lack of eye contact sends off signals that the person is not much interested in the ongoing conversation. Women use more eye contact compared to men. Because they are emotional beings, women know that eye contact creates more connections between two people; hence, they do it more often. They also know that it creates a sense of trust and security, which is important to most of them when they have conversations.

Men, nevertheless, would not be bothered much by eye contact. As long as they can hear you and offer his contribution to the conversation, they would be fine. It takes practice and understanding the importance of eye contact for them to do it. The majority don't take it as a big deal; the main reason why some relationships suffer. Eye contact is essential in most settings, and it has been proven to be a sign of confidence and trust, which is something everyone should endeavor to do.

Listening: Women believe that eye contact is a sign of listening and being interested in a conversation. Because of this, they are mostly able to maintain eye contact in a conversation or when listening to someone. It does make a lot of sense. However, men are less likely to associate eye contact with listening. A man will look on the side or focus on something else in the room, but still be attentive and listen to what one is saying. Some do listen this way while looking a bit distant, but then offer solutions to a problem at hand, and that is when one will know they were actually listening. Just because some avoid eye contact does not mean they are poor listeners. It just proves that they do it differently and need more understanding to be on the same page.

Variation in body language: This is a major communication factor in any kind of setting, whether in a relationship or not. It differs among women and men, as they each have different understandings of what certain body languages mean.

Women are highly expressive and will use a lot of hand waving, move their bodies in a certain way when talking to certain people, or just use a lot of gestures when conversing. We can say women can be more animated in their conversations compared to men.

Men are always a lot more calmers and show less emotion. They will stand in one posture or sit up straight and not make any movements, as they think it portrays them as being in control of their emotions. As women struggle to get attention to them when talking, men would want to avoid it altogether.

Verbal Communication

When it comes to talking, there is still a big difference between men and women. The majority of women will talk a lot while men mostly take it easy and try to internalize situations first. Also, men might want to talk only when necessary, while women would have no issue talking more and more. There are some instances where men talk more than women (depending on personality), but this is not very common.

Paralanguage: This is mostly about intonation, pitch, speed of speaking, etc. It does happen to both genders, but it is more pronounced in women than in men. Men are more likely to listen and do a lot of nodding to show agreement, while women will most likely make sounds on top of body movement to show they are engaged in the conversation. About intonation, women take it more seriously to be able to get their feelings and emotions in the speech, unlike men who are more straightforward. Women will say "yes" or "mmh" as they listen to someone talking, as a sign of agreement or to indicate that they are following the conversation, while men with be quiet and still follow it through.

Emotional expressivity: It is common knowledge that women are emotional beings. Because of that, they also express their emotions a lot. Most women want their emotional state to be taken care of for them to find the relationship fulfilling. If they have a bad day, they will want to talk to their man about it, not for any solution, but just for their emotional stability. When stressed, women would talk about it more and feel relieved and happy. This is the reason why most are happy when they are shown affection and attention because it deals with their emotions.

Men, however, are not much concerned with emotions. They are more of a realist than emotional. They would rather deal with an issue head-on and think of the solution or way forward instead of crying about it. It actually is the total opposite, as men are more likely to recede in a cocoon when stressed. The majority prefer to deal with their issues inwardly rather than letting it out and talking about it with no clear solution.

Women, on the other hand, being emotional, would most of the time, use hints and not say it as it is. This is because they would mostly not want to hurt their partner's feelings. It is helpful, but then it leaves them frustrated and not satisfied. Some will also just get moody, and it will be the man's responsibility to know out what would be bothering them. This makes it very difficult for some people in relationships, hence the importance of learning to communicate and knowing what works for each individual.

Chapter 2: The Four Stages Of Love

According to psychologists and scholars of couples' relationships, love relationships go through four stages: infatuation, falling in love, disillusionment, and lasting love. In reality, many couples do not go through the third stage of the relationship, which is the most critical. Knowing these stages is important because, depending on the season in which the couple lives, it is possible to provide appropriate care so the love grows and does not wither.

Infatuation

This is the most beautiful stage of love: we feel happy and believe we have found the right person for us. We cannot even conceive of the idea of not loving our partner: we project all our dreams and desires onto them. We think that, after the disappointments of the past, our time has come to be happy and to have found eternal love. We value our partner's merits to the nth degree and completely set aside their faults.

There is a scientific explanation for all this: hormones such as serotonin, testosterone, estrogen, dopamine, and oxytocin affect our mind.

At this stage, it is very often that, in our mind, reality surpasses all hope and dreams: it is all wonderful.

In reality, the stage of infatuation can be the result of chance and there is no guarantee that you have found your soulmate. Sometimes, ideally unsuitable couples are formed rationally. This is because, in this stage, the emotional and unconscious element prevails. This stage can generally last from a single day (in the case of an obvious blunder) to eighteen months. Usually the couple passes this stage.

Falling in love

This is the stage in which the real couple is born: usually you go to live together, you are happy to share everything, you feel safe and pampered by your partner. Respect and esteem grow reciprocally, and you start to build, to make plans together: an individual thought is flanked by a "couple" thought.

In this amorous season there is no doubt that the initial enthusiasm will subside, leading to a more objective view of the couple. In any case, it is based on a more solid and rational bond: you continue to value the qualities of the other person and the defects are overcome by the right compromises. At this stage, the couple is happy and hopeful that this will last forever.

This cycle generally lasts until the seventh year and, being a positive stage for the couple, it is easy to reach the third cycle of love.

Disillusionment

Generally, after the seventh year of the couple's existence, we reach the negative stage of disillusionment: we realize the partner is a human being with their own strengths and weaknesses; we feel less loved and do not want to give the love that was given in the other stages of the relationship; past wounds re-emerge and affect the balance of the couple; we do not feel fulfilled and, in some cases, we feel chained to the partner.

This stage accentuates the tendency of men to shut themselves up in silence and appear detached; at the same time, the tendency of women, at times, to be pessimistic and to see a dark and unhappy future is also accentuated.

This, unfortunately, is the stage in which many couples do not survive. There is not the will to work to build a solid and lasting love.

This is the stage in which both must struggle to understand the needs of the other person and ask for the help they need.

Love is a militia: you must build, be lovable day by day; this is the only way to build true love.

This guide is intended to help couples to overcome negative moments, to make feelings flourish again with the right strategies and to build a lasting love.

Lasting love

Not all couples will reach this stage, but for those that will, the benefits and satisfactions will be the highest: the partner is not the ideal savior we believed in the cycle of infatuation, but an ally who helped soothe the inner conflicts of the past, who loves us for who we are, with our virtues and flaws. The partner is a rock: the friend, the lover, the dearest person. Their support will never be lacking because they love us and know us deeply.

This is the stage in which you can have bliss and live intensely the love bond that was built with so much love. It is such a beautiful feeling you want to share it with others.

If two people have managed to build such a beautiful relationship, they want to project their happiness onto others, contributing to building a better world. The couple will leave a trail of light in the world.

The beginnings of a relationship

Let's assume you are in the early stages of a relationship. The first aspect to define is whether you want to commit yourself seriously to building something important with that person or not. Not everyone wants to build something serious and solid: sometimes you have other priorities, like career or fun; sometimes the other person is not ready.

Therefore, you have to try to understand if you and your partner are on the same wavelength and have the desire to build a solid and lasting relationship.

If the answer to the above question is yes, you need to define what key characteristics the partner must have to meet your expectations.

Then you need to know yourself: you need to understand your priorities, your values and the compromises you are willing to make; if these elements are clear to you, it will be easier for the person next to you to understand and respect them.

You then have to find out if you have the main life goals in common: love, work, sharing, and children.

You have to be aware that you will go through several difficulties and you have to be willing to overcome them with courage, tenacity and with the awareness that, once overcome, they will help to strengthen the relationship.

You should also consider that there are substantial differences between the life of a single person and the life of a couple; some are obvious, others are more subtle.

To live peacefully an engagement or a marriage, you need to review your habits, have the ability to adapt to the new status and be willing to accept the changes that have occurred.

If you have been single for many years, it is likely you will find it a little more difficult to adapt to change as you are used to your schedules, your habits, your hobbies, your friendships, without having to compromise with anyone. If you are a certain age and still live blissfully with your parents, adapting to change will require even more effort.

That does not mean you have to turn your pre-relationship life upside down. You have to remain consistent with your values; maintain some hobbies you care about; maintain your friendships.

This last element is fundamental: never neglect friendships. From personal experience, I can say that I have lived through dozens of relationships, even lasting ones: sometimes I ended the relationship; other times I was left. In all this, historical friendships have always been a fundamental point of reference in my life. In the most important moments of my existence, I have always had friends who have supported and cheered me up.

Therefore, it is necessary to change your habits, dedicating to the couple the time they deserve, but it is also necessary to carve out room for yourself.

As I mentioned above, the first step is to decide what kind of relationship you want to live in.

In this regard, the advice I want to give you is never to rush things: take the time to understand if that person is on your wavelength. One mistake many people make is to settle for and mate with the wrong person just out of loneliness or age. This is a huge mistake because a couple's relationship can be wonderful, but it can turn into the anteroom of hell, so it is better to be alone than live a destructive relationship.

Therefore, dismiss any decisions made based on emergency, fear and in a period of low self-esteem, and think that the right person for you will come at the right time and in unexpected ways and means.

If in a couple's relationship you find that there are often misunderstandings, incompatible character differences, completely different values, then stop and take your time.

If the relationship you are in does not satisfy you, psychologically traps you and does not make you happy, it is better to end it at the beginning, or before the wedding.

If you end a destructive relationship before it becomes too demanding, the pain and regret will be shorter and the breakup will involve fewer people; in the case of a more serious relationship, it will also affect families, mutual friendships and any children.

It is physiological that if you are trying to build a new, serious, and lasting relationship, you will have to face some difficulties. However, these small problems and difficulties will help you understand how willing you are to accept the other person. If your partner overreacts to small difficulties, and the slightest misunderstanding turns into a tragedy, then I advise you to end the relationship immediately.

I want to talk to you about an experience I had about ten years ago.

I was in a period of low self-esteem: I was no longer in my twenties and many family members were beginning to ask me why I was not engaged or married. So, I got engaged to a girl with a good job and a good reputation. Over time, however, I realized that she was too authoritarian: she wanted to decide for herself about our life; she wanted me to abandon my historical friendships; she even wanted me to change my values and my way of thinking.

I was not happy with her and, although in the eyes of the family we had what it takes to get married, I kept putting it off, year after year. Meanwhile, my grudge and resentment towards my partner increased. One day she gave me an ultimatum and asked me when I wanted to get married. With no hesitation, I answered her that I was never going to do it: it was a good decision!

If, on the other hand, you feel that the relationship completely satisfies you, makes you happy and fulfilled, that you get along well, have similar tastes and personalities, then follow your emotional side and without fear build something important! A few months are enough to understand if she or he is the right person.

With my authoritarian ex-girlfriend, I hesitated for years to build something important because we were not on the same wavelength.

However, when I met my wife, I immediately understood that she was my soulmate: she is a beautiful Belarusian, sweet and understanding, we have the same values and goals. I am happy with her. I will not hide the fact that we got married after only seeing each other three times. It was, for my part, the wisest decision of my life! Now, when I wake up in the morning, I often contemplate the blond angel next to me, our sweet children and the day starts with a radiant smile.

The second step, as I mentioned above, is to know yourself. This important aspect should not be underestimated: it is essential that you not only know your virtues and qualities, but also your flaws and any limits that block you. Only in this way, can you begin a path of personal growth, so you can overcome these limits and improve both individually and within the couple.

When you really learn to know yourself, you can express who you are with more confidence and freedom and this will allow your partner to accept you as you really are.

Many people try to appear in a different way than they really are, and this is not good for the relationship because the very essence of the relationship cannot be considered authentic.

Seduction strategies — sometimes including lies or tricks — can only serve in the approach phase to stimulate the emotional side of the future partner. However, if you want to build the relationship on a solid and lasting basis you have to be sincere and authentic. To do this, you first need to get to know each other.

I advise that you learn to observe the other person with curiosity and interest, to ask specific questions and to listen carefully to their answers. In this way, you can penetrate the personality of your loved one. Some people, mistakenly, concentrate on talking without properly listening to their partner. However, keep in mind that when you talk, you say things you already know, while it is when you listen that you can discover and understand new things and the relationship can be strengthened.

The third step is to understand if you share common goals: the will to live together, to love each other, to respect each other, to share the same values. To understand this, you need to take time to understand and get to know each other.

If you notice right from the start of a relationship that there is no sense of protection, if there is no genuine love, if you see that the other person is not completely present, or is only partially interested in things that concern you, do not expect that these things will change with the passage of time.

On the contrary, as we have already seen, over time these failings may even increase. The enthusiasm on the part of the other person, the sense of happiness is fundamental and must be present in the first encounters.

The factors underlying a happy and satisfying relationship are few, but they are essential: their absence indicates the other person is probably not ready to commit himself or herself completely or that he or she does not intend to engage in a serious and lasting relationship. In this case, the relationship should be ended without delay.

Chapter 3: Understanding Jealousy

Jealousy

Jealousy is a complex emotion that encompasses feelings ranging from suspicion to rage to fear of humiliation. It strikes people of all ages, genders, and sexual orientations, and is most typically aroused when a person perceives a threat to a valued relationship from a third party. The threat may be real or imagined. Jealousy generally refers to the thoughts or feelings of insecurity, fear, and concern over a relative lack of possessions or safety.

Jealousy can consist of one or more emotions such as anger, resentment, inadequacy, helplessness, or disgust. In its original meaning, jealousy is distinct from envy, though the two terms have popularly become synonymous in the English language, with jealousy now also taking on the definition originally used for envy alone. Jealousy, like anger, is what is known as a secondary emotion, in that it surfaces as a response to another deeper emotion that resides underneath it. If you follow your jealousy down and ask it why it has come to visit you, you'll usually find either hurt or fear underneath. Follow the 'why' down, several layers, and you will find your answer.

Fear-Based Example: "I feel jealous because my boyfriend still engages with the female BFF that he used to date. Why does this bother me? Because a part of me fears that she will make a move on him and threaten our relationship. So fear is the culprit. Has my partner ever given me any reason to doubt him? No. Then what is the more truthful, empowering statement to hold on to? I trust my partner implicitly, I know that he loves me, and I know that I have nothing to worry about. I should report my mind to my partner, owning my emotions entirely, to remove this falsely perceived block between us."

Hurt-Based Example: "I feel jealous that my girlfriend spends so much time out with her friends after work. Why does this bother me? Because she does this often enough that I feel like she doesn't place me as a priority in her life. Okay, any other reason? Yes, one time she stayed out late and ended up getting drunk and making out with a guy that she didn't know. So there is unresolved hurt... were amends made? Do I feel safe with her or do we need to discuss this further to feel safe in our relationship? I don't feel safe, we need to discuss it more so that we can move forward more healthily."

If your jealousy is pointing towards old unresolved HURT from past transgressions, then that needs to be addressed and you are within your rights to ask that things shift so that you feel safer in your relationship.

If your jealousy is pointing you towards your FEAR, then you need to embrace the truth of the situation and come to a more reality-based version of your internal story, as opposed to being controlled by your mind.

"Jealousy is conceptualized as a cognitive, emotional, and behavioral response to a relationship threat. In the case of sexual jealousy, this threat emanates from knowing or suspecting that one's partner has had (or desires to have) sexual activity with a third party. In the case of emotional jealousy, an individual feels threatened by her or his partner's emotional involvement with and/or love for a third party."

"Jealousy is defined as a defensive reaction to a perceived threat to a valued relationship, arising from a situation in which the partner's involvement with an activity and/or another person is contrary to the jealous person's definition of their relationship."

"Jealousy is triggered by the threat of separation from, or loss of, a romantic partner when that threat is attributed to the possibility of the partner's romantic interest in another person."

The Common Experience Of Jealousy For Many People May Involve:

- Fear of loss

- Suspicion of or anger about a perceived betrayal
- Low self-esteem and sadness over perceived loss
- Uncertainty and loneliness
- Fear of losing an important person to another
- Distrust

The Experience Of Envy Involves:
- Feelings of inferiority
- Longing
- Resentment of circumstances
- Motivation to improve
- Desire to possess the attractive rival's qualities
- Disapproval of feelings
- Sadness towards other's accomplishments

Jealousy involves an entire "emotional episode," including a complex "narrative": the circumstances that lead up to jealousy, jealousy itself as emotion, any attempt at self-regulation, subsequent actions and events, and the resolution of the episode.

The narrative can originate from experienced facts, thoughts, perceptions, memories, but also imagination, guess, and assumptions. The more society and culture matter in the formation of these factors, the more jealousy can have a social and cultural origin. By contrast, jealousy can be a "cognitively impenetrable state", where education and rational belief matter very little.

Romantic Jealousy

Romantic jealousy arises as a result of romantic interest. When the romantic advances of a young heterosexual male are always rejected and ignored by a lot of young women that he considers very attractive then the continued "rejection" or disinterest by those women can cause the male to feel jealousy and feelings of grief and might even trigger severe depression and in some cases, even the desire to end one's life. And throughout history, countless women and men have even ended their life because of countless romantic rejections.

It is defined as "a complex of thoughts, feelings, and actions that follow threats to self-esteem and/or threats to the existence or quality of the relationship when those threats are generated by the perception of a real or potential romantic attraction between one's partner and a (perhaps imaginary) rival. Different from sexual jealousy, romantic jealousy is triggered by threats to self and relationship (rather than sexual interest in another person). Factors, such as feelings of inadequacy as a partner, sexual exclusivity, and having put relatively more effort into the relationship, are positively related to relationship jealousy in both genders.

Sexual Jealousy

Sexual jealousy may be triggered when a person's significant other displays a sexual interest in another person. The feeling of jealousy may be just as powerful if one partner suspects the other is guilty of infidelity. Fearing that their partner will experience sexual jealousy the unfaithful person may lie about their actions to protect their partner. Experts often believe that sexual jealousy is a biological imperative. It may be part of a mechanism by which humans and other animals ensure access to the best reproductive partners.

It seems that male jealousy in heterosexual relationships may be influenced by their female partner's phase in her menstrual cycle. In the period around and shortly before ovulation, males are found to display more mate-retention tactics, which are linked to jealousy. Furthermore, a male is more likely to employ mate-retention tactics if their partner shows more interest in other males, which is more likely to occur in the pre-ovulation phase.

Why We Feel Jealous

Jealousy is often thought of in the context of romantic relationships: a boyfriend who forbids his girlfriend from talking to other men, for instance, or a person who can't stand to see her old flame post pictures with a new partner on Facebook. But the feeling can occur in almost every type of human relationship from siblings competing for parental attention to coworkers trying to impress a respected boss.

Although jealousy is a painful emotional experience, evolutionary psychologists regard it not as an emotion to be suppressed but as one to heed as a signal or a wake-up call that a valued relationship is in danger and that steps need to be taken to regain the affection of a mate or friend. As a result, jealousy is seen as a necessary emotion, because it preserves social bonds and motivates people to engage in behaviors that maintain important relationships.

Why Am I So Jealous?

I have identified many root causes of extreme jealousy, including low self-esteem, high neuroticism, and feeling possessive of others, particularly romantic partners. Fear of abandonment is also a key motivator.

re Men More Jealous Than Women?

Men and women both feel jealous. Some evidence suggests that in the context of romantic relationships, men feel greater jealousy about sexual infidelity (real or perceived), while women tend to feel more jealous about emotional infidelity.

Is Jealousy Good Or Bad For Relationships? Unwarranted jealousy often causes relationship unrest or dissatisfaction, and jealous people can behave in ways that are unreasonable or even dangerous. But jealousy is a natural, adaptive feeling designed to preserve important relationships. Feeling jealous may signal a relationship's value or that two people are drifting apart.

Envy, Compersion, And Other Related Feelings

Jealousy and envy are similar feelings, but they're not the same. Jealousy always involves a third party seen as a rival for affection or attention. Envy occurs between only two people and is best summed up as, "I want what you have." For example, someone may feel envious of another's wealth, status, or appearance.

Compersion is another feeling loosely related to romantic or sexual jealousy. Compersion occurs when, rather than feeling distressed that a partner is emotionally or sexually involved with someone else, the individual feels happy for them. Compersion is most often discussed in the context of polyamory and other consensually non-monogamous relationships.

What Should I Do If I Feel Envious Of My Partner?

Be honest about your feelings and work to directly address any underlying issues (such as inequality within the relationship or personal feelings of inadequacy). It may help for the envious partner to pursue concrete avenues such as a career change or a new workout routine—to boost self-efficacy and self-esteem.

How Often Have You Experienced Envy For Something Missing In Your Life?

It could be due to lack of money, limited material possessions, not having healthy relationships, or lack of attention from someone important to you. Maybe you're jealous of someone who seems to have the things you crave for, a lifestyle you aspire to or even a physique you've always longed for, but don't seem to be able to achieve.

Where Does Jealousy Come From?

Often there is a concrete "trigger" for jealousy, coupled with experience from the past and/or the history of the partner.

An unknown number on the mobile phone display, looks, too long conversations, the business trip, or supposedly groundless overtime, previously cheated or knowing that the partner used to be unfaithful in other relationships.

The cause, however, is to look elsewhere, in the past of the jealous person.

Often, the reasons for jealousy are in childhood. Lack of attention from the parents can be a cause of jealousy, but also sibling rivalry and the feeling of being subordinated to it. Due to a lack of time or disinterest, a deficit has already been created here. Those who grew up with siblings and always had to compete for the favor of their parents are more susceptible to jealousy than single children who have grown up in stable and loving relationships.

Even those who had to watch one parent in childhood cheat the other often develop a disturbed trust in their relationships. The experiences in one's love relationships can also play a significant role in the development of jealousy. Actual breaches of trust due to cheating as well as own infidelity, but also the devaluation of the person can lead to less faith in oneself and the partner.

You Can Contain Your Jealousy

You have realized that you are always jealous and the fact it strains your relationship? That's already an important step. Realize, in reality, you doubt more yourself and your values than your partner's behavior.

You First Have To Learn To Accept This Fact For Yourself

With practice, you can accept your feelings and transform them with empathy, compassion for yourself. It strengthens the trust in your partner and especially in you. It's also helpful to bring the partner on board and to ask for help to get jealousy under control.

Ask Yourself The Following questions

- Did your partner cheat on you?
- Are there any people in your partner's life who are more attractive to your partner than you are?
- Have you ever been betrayed in previous relationships? What do you think was the reason?
- Have you been jealous of all your relationships so far?
- Do you have siblings, or are you an only child?
- Have you witnessed infidelity with your parents?
- Did your parents give you insufficient attention (in your eyes)? But for the siblings, other children, people, or activities?
- Have you been taught in your past that you are not lovable or good enough?
- Do beliefs have formed in you like "For me, there is no real love." Or "Nobody stays with me. Everyone leaves me. "?

There may be more than one point on the list. Once you have identified the topic that leads to your jealousy, you should try to process and conclude it. Depending on the severity, some open discussions will help you a bit further, but it can also make sense to have therapy.

What you should first learn is to recognize your amiability. The key to winning over jealousy is self-acceptance, which is entirely independent of your partner or other people. This independence is generally important. What if your beloved partner or another important person were gone tomorrow? After all, you can also lose someone in other ways than to someone else. Your jealousy is also not a "proof" of love. Make sure that you always be able to stand on your own feet.

Independence has nothing to do with the fact that you value your partner less or don't need love or partnership. It is the basis for a healthy love relationship. The behavioral patterns that constrict your partner or trample on his privacy should be discarded. After all, you also expect respect for your privacy, even when there is nothing to hide. It is essential that you again learn to trust. Become aware that you can't control everything and often hide future fears behind coined fears from your past.

Understand Your Jealous Partner

If your partner is always without cause and/or pathological jealousy, your coexistence suffers. But as long as you haven't given an objectively understandable reason for jealousy, there is nothing that you could do or change or could you?

To improve the situation, you can actively seek the conversation. Take the initiative and bring the topic "jealousy" to the table. Most importantly, avoid any allegations, accusations, and anything that could make your partner feel like you're pointing fingers because this would strengthen the already existing self-doubt and fear of losing even more.

It Is Better To Ask questions

- Which situations trigger jealousy?
- Does jealousy refer only to certain people?
- What's going on in the head of the jealous?

- What experiences in past relationships "justify" jealousy?
- Did you have moments of rejection or abandonment in your childhood?
- Did the parents exemplify a pattern of insecurity?

By asking these questions, you can show that you are seriously interested in clarifying the situation and at the same time show genuine interest in the partner. It can be a great help that your partner feels that you are serious about him/her. Moreover, these mental impulses open up the possibility of self-reflection on the causes of his jealousy. If he is open to it, he may in future evaluate situations that cause jealousy in him differently.

Once you have found out the causes, develop a plan with him/her for how to work together to reduce jealousy. Of course, this plan must have a structure. For example, it would be unhealthy if you reveal everything, or you can no longer move freely in your life. It is unhealthy for you to be dominated by the fear of another and to develop your fear of the fear of your partner (and what he/she is doing for his / her dismay). That's the sure way into a co-dependency. To maintain harmony at all costs, from one's fear of conflict, sadness, and anger of the partner, silence as punishment or other measures of the partner to express oneself emotionally, is not helpful. We are all grown up and need to learn urgently, especially when dealing with onerous feelings if we have previously suppressed them. That's not only feasible but also useful for the rest of your life. Essential insight for yourself maybe that the attacks of jealousy are not from evil will, but from loss anxiety even if supposedly a power game in the foreground. The exercise of power too often results from an underlying uncertainty. But make it clear to your partner in conversation that now and then like every human being in a healthy, functioning relationship you have to delineate yourself and need free space.

What Drives You To Experience Jealousy And Is It Something We Can Control?

Feelings of envy quite often start in early childhood, maybe when a child feels their sibling is getting more praise or attention from a parent. Or it could be when a child has or is given a toy or possession that is wanted by their sibling but denied it. Quite often these feelings are criticized as bad behavior and the situation is left unexplained which can cause anxiety, resentment, and confusion for the child. If parents are displaying envious feelings, these emotions can be understood by their children to be acceptable normal behavior. As a result, they may learn to have these negative tendencies as they are growing up and into adulthood. Negative behavior from your parents or other bad experiences in childhood can cause low self-esteem and make you feel unloved and unworthy. These emotions also trigger feelings of insecurity which can cause jealousy.

Jealousy is not a rare emotion - many people feel it occasionally. It can tear your relationships apart and raise all sorts of negative emotions - resentment, insecurity, mistrust, and low self-esteem, to name a few. It can also be a sign that it's time to change something in your life that will allow you to move on to a more healthy, self-fulfilling, positive phase. Rather than letting jealousy affect your relationships with others, use it as a reason to understand yourself and the fears that cause it.

The Emotions Of Jealousy

Jealousy is a combination of fear and anger, often fed by the fear of losing someone (or a cherished situation/state of affairs) and anger that someone else is taking control of your involvement with the person or situation that is so important to you. It's a destructive and negative emotion that can make you feel worthless and fearful. Recognition of this powerful emotion is your number one self-defense. Once you've identified your feelings, try to understand why you're feeling jealous. Often jealousy is about reliving an experience of failure from the past that continues to affect your level of trust (or lack of) toward people in the present, even though current conditions may be vastly different. Other motivators for feeling jealous include a high level of insecurity, vulnerability, anger towards yourself, and fear of abandonment. If you're honest with yourself, you will realize that jealous feeling often occur at the same time you feel threatened, afraid of being abandoned, or when you feel you just cannot trust the other person, no matter how little basis your lack of trust has. However, this self-realization shouldn't be just about finding fault with yourself - being compassionate about your self-assessment is an essential part of staying objective about the green-eyed monster. Remember this emotion isn't a sign of failure or bad character, but probably just the result of previous experiences or learned behavior when you were growing up.

Face Your Feelings Now

Learn to question your jealousy every time that it emerges. For example, say to yourself "Is this jealously because I feel afraid or angry? Why am I feeling fear or anger?" When you begin to question what makes you jealous at the moment, you can begin to take positive steps to manage the feelings constructively, without the cloud of negative emotion that typically accompanies jealousy. Questions you can ask yourself are:

- What is making me feel jealous?
- Why am I feeling jealous about this?
- Why do I feel threatened?
- What am I trying to hold on to, should I just let it go?

Change Any False Beliefs That Might Be Fuelling Your Jealousy

There are often false, baseless beliefs that underlie reactions of jealousy. If you examine and can understand the belief, you can often eliminate the jealousy. Some common underlying beliefs without basis include "Everyone is out to get me".

If I don't achieve x, y or z, then I will be a failure". "If this person leaves me, I must be unworthy and won't meet someone else". These are generalizations that could never be applied to every person you know or meet. These are pre-emptive defenses against the possibility of something bad happening to you. Beliefs are changeable by choice. If you change your belief, you can change the way you feel. Choose to tell yourself a belief that is nurturing and supportive, and you'll feel better. If your default is to think negatively, ask yourself what possible benefit that brings you overthinking positively. Thoughts create emotions and you have the choice to make the thoughts negative or positive. When you begin taking steps to create a happy and fulfilling life for yourself, you will find the anger and fear easier to manage, removing the fuel which creates jealous emotions.

Be aware that your thoughts can happen so quickly that you may not even realize consciously that you've had a negative thought. Developing a greater awareness of your thoughts and what triggers them is a large part of tackling the problem. Every time a negative thought comes into your head, immediately try to banish it and think of a positive one. If you let negative thoughts dwell, you will perpetuate this emotion and more negative thoughts will follow. Try to get into the habit of pushing them out of your mind as soon as they occur and you will be surprised at how much better you feel, you will be happier and other people will react more positively towards you.

Communicate Your Feelings

Discuss your feelings of jealousy with the person who is causing them. Sharing your true feelings and talking it through can be a very cathartic and constructive way to start mending the damage. It can also be a way of creating an ally, someone who will feel able to point out when you make unreasonable jealous demands on him or her without expecting a comeback. During these discussions, consider the following:

☐ Avoid passing on the blame to the other person. His or her behavior is not the cause of your feelings - you are responsible for your feelings.

☐ Stick to "I" statements rather than saying "you make me feel…". Instead of saying "You shouldn't have done that", say "I felt terrible when that happened."

☐ Be aware that how you perceive situations may be completely different from how the other person sees them. Stay as open-minded as possible, even though this will probably mean that you sometimes feel extremely defensive. Try to keep quiet and listen rather than constantly interrupting with justifications

☐ Above all, be compassionate, both for yourself and for the person you've been offloading your jealousy onto. Recognize the harm your feelings have caused them and you, and work together to find a better way forward. Be passionate about your desire to improve your feelings and try to outgrow jealousy

☐ In most cases, this won't be a one-off conversation. You may need to agree to talk any time your jealous emotions appear.

Remember Jealousy Is About You, Not The Other Person

Bear in mind at all times that feelings of jealousy are about you, not about the other person. Any sense that things are out of control means that you need to transfer the intensity of what you're feeling into something constructive rather than continuing to over-analyze the relationship (or situation). For example, get involved in an activity may be a sport or some other exercise, a hobby, or participate in volunteer work. Do something that takes you out of yourself and causes you to focus beyond the relationship or situation and gives you an outlet for your emotions that is healthy and not be ruminating and raising suspicions.

Learn From Your Jealousy

Negative emotions can have a role in shaping our lives, for teaching each of us how to be a better person and for struggling to overcome them. They have a place and not just one that controls you and causes unwelcome behavior. Some of the things jealousy might teach you to include:

1. Dealing With New Relationships

You are frightened when a relationship is new and still has some way to go before it feels secure. This is a commonplace feeling in young relationships for many people, and both possessiveness, as well as a sense of vulnerability at getting close to someone, can drive feelings of jealousy (testing our power can become a very harmful pastime)

2. Trusting Your Partner

You feel your partner has a roving eye. In romantic relationships, both men and women continue to 'check out' other men and women. It's biologically driven and it's natural. However, in the majority of cases, it does not mean that the person wants to leave the relationship he or she is in with you or that they think someone else looks or is better than you. It is, for most people, about appreciating the human form and not about a roaming eye. This misunderstanding has long created unnecessary jealousy as long as relationships have existed. It can help to accept that it's okay for a person in a committed relationship to look, provided they don't touch! The fact that they feel able to look at other people when they are with you may demonstrate how open and honest they are and feel they don't have anything to hide.

3. People Envy

Other people may have material possessions, relationships, or a lifestyle that you don't have but would like. It's a very natural reaction to feel envious of these people, even if they are close to you. You also have the additional problem of hiding these negative emotions from them. These feelings can create resentment that will in time affect your relationships and how feel about that person. To justify your jealousy, you may try to convince yourself that this person is unworthy, not a good person, or undeserving of such riches. Remember they have not created your feelings of jealousy towards them, you have. That it's our life circumstances that determine how much we have or don't have, however unfair or unjust it sometimes appears to be. Try to view this situation positively, admire their achievements as something to aspire to, however difficult that may feel. Acknowledge that we are all the same and capable of attracting personal riches into our lives, however big or small.

4. Ability Insecurity

You're afraid someone else will take your job, salary, role, position, etc. In this case, you're probably afraid of financial insecurity (survival instinct) or you feel that you're an impostor in your role, the latter an all-too-commonly held false belief in many high-achieving people in the workforce. Remember that you wouldn't have been given the role or position unless other people felt you were capable and had earned it (don't be your own worst enemy), or be scared of being 'found out' that you feel you might not be 'up to the job'. Try living up to that trust in you rather than seeing demons hovering in every corner. Remember that only you know how you are truly feeling. You may lack confidence, but that fact may not be apparent to anyone else. We all can 'mask our feelings' sometimes without even realizing it.

5. Confidence In Your Beliefs

You listen to people who say mean or exaggerated things and let this direct your emotions. Take a stand! Be true to yourself and those you love. All too common, many people are easily convinced by local gossip because it sounds so compelling and seems like it must be true. The reality is that it's rarely right and it's always far better not to listen to people who chatter away with idle gossip, making things up as they go. Believe in facts, not fiction! If something doesn't feel or sound right, it usually isn't - trust your instincts.

6. Facing Up To Facts

You feel uncomfortable looking within yourself and working through difficult emotions. You ignore the problem rather than do the hard work of facing your emotions and dealing with them internally. Jealousy is painful but by facing it, you can repair much internal damage, make your relationships stronger and more enduring, and ultimately feel better about yourself.

Trust Yourself

Trust begins at home - with yourself! If you learn to trust and believe in yourself, you can radiate this trust onto others. Begin by making a list of all your good points. Put this list up somewhere you can see it often, to remind you that you're already fully equipped with good qualities, great talent, and personable skills. Only compare yourself to yourself - not to others, try to focus on your achievements and pursuits without worrying what other people are doing or thinking.

Remind yourself daily, maybe through a journal, affirmations, or another effective way, that you have what it takes to be successful and emotionally fulfilled in life. Practicing healthy thinking must be a daily, recurring action - it involves continual practice. In time, the healthier thinking processes will take over the destructive ones and help you to become a whole person, resilient, capable, and not prone to jealous thoughts.

☐Work on relevant aspects of your self-esteem if you feel it's lacking. When you have more confidence in yourself and your relationships, you'll be less likely to feel jealous.

- Use your jealousy to be a better person, to face up to past demons and anxieties that may still be haunting you. Work through old negative emotions and eliminate them from your current thinking.
- Read some self-help books on jealousy and you'll feel you're getting to grips on how to manage and eventually banish this negative emotion.

Negative Consequences Of Unmanaged Emotions

Jealous man of a woman textingOvercoming jealousy is a myth. There is no real need to overcome anything. What we need to do is accept our feelings as legitimate guides. When we understand jealousy from a perspective of desired growth, we can identify precisely our desires. If we diffuse the strong charge that usually accompanies envy, we can search for what triggered the emotion. Once we pinpoint the area where we feel lack, we can then decide whether we are committed to fulfilling our desires and working toward the desired outcome.

Some Common Fears That Ignite Jealousy

- The unknown or a major change
- A loss or an imagined catastrophe
- Protection from feeling hurt
- Feeling inadequate or having a lack of self-esteem or confidence
- Fear of losing a valued relationship or the rejection by someone we love

Negative Aspects Of Unmanaged Jealousy

- Often creates hurt, fatigue, anxiety, anger, and sometimes irrational actions.
- Jealousy is rooted in fear, not self-worth or power, which disempowers a person through a belief that others have something he or she cannot have.
- Fear that others will steal what is important to the person.
- Fuels mistrust and increases distance in relationships.
- Depletes positive energy toward goals.
- Robs the person from an opportunity of self-development when the emotion goes unheard.

Positive Aspects Of Listening To Our Emotions

- Offers an opportunity to imagine and claim what we are capable of having, doing, and being.
- Shows us where we have stunted our personal growth.
- Increases gratitude for our unlimited potential to create a life we love.
- Provides the opportunity to acknowledge weak areas of trust in ourselves and our relationships so closeness can increase.
- Signals us that a boundary is needed or that we need to advocate for ourselves.

How To Effectively Handle Jealousy

The first step is awareness when we seek to navigate this emotion. Stop and acknowledge what you're feeling. Let go of the tug of war. Stop fighting the feeling. Replace negative mental chatter that makes you feel worse with encouraging and soothing self-talk. Relax and move to acceptance. Emotions are intended to help us process our experiences so we can be our best selves. Own and accept what you feel; your feelings are there to guide you to your truth. Each emotion is a messenger of your values, needs, and desires. Being able to process and work through difficult feelings helps you grow emotionally. Every time you feel an emotion, you open up the flow, unfreezing energy that is trapped.

Emotions show us how to course correct flawlessly if we listen and act on their wisdom. When you take the time to work through painful experiences and their accompanying emotions, the experience is integrated, and you develop a sense of inner peace within yourself. And when you are at peace, you have much more energy for pursuing what's important to you. Inner peace allows you to love yourself and others more freely. To accomplish this outcome, we must be willing to acknowledge all of our emotions and feelings and be open to exploring them.

Chapter 4: The Relationship Life Cycle

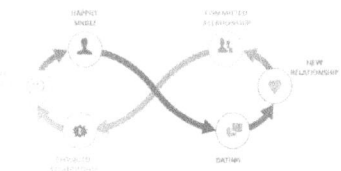

The Relationship Cycle

"Every good relationship, especially marriage, is based on respect. If it's not based on respect, nothing that appears to be good will last very long. – Amy Grant

The principle has been true, and businesses have actually got a grip on how goods come and go on the market.

The history taught everyone to look at the deal between the customer and the seller and conclude that that was the "end game." There we do not use the term 'relationship' for a crucial reason, which is evident at a time. It is enough to claim that the "transaction" was one case at a time when a product or service changed hands when a payment was received.

The consumer life cycle provided a way for a retailer to view a client not just as a single transaction, but as an ongoing service supplier throughout its lifespan. Salesmen were urged to classify policy as the ultimate long-term sequence of activities that cover the whole set of transactions where a particular consumer would influence rather than treating a client as a sequence of "one-off" orders. We also switched from "selling" to "reaching the needs of our clients."

Both were customer-centered, but the latter style powered much more customer service. The first result was a change in the order taking process, which led to more sensitive, cautious, and ready touches on the client in the expectation that the same buyer would come to the retailer for more sales.

All product and consumer life cycle processes are one-way, in that the "consumer is sovereign" and that the retailer has little or no role in the perception of consumers and their needs. In other words, the Consumer Life Cycle never even goes past the sheer aggravation of the importance of all orders obtained in life (in this case, the customer or the seller).

The advantages of consumer attention that have contributed to the consumer life cycle are more reliable than any set of covert, discrete product life cycle "transaction" procedures may have. Due to the one-directional flow of information, however, some significant advantages remain on the table. To order to steal the lead in the supply chain race, the most ambitious and creative businesses needed to build a partnership life cycle.

Life-cycle and Relationship-Cycles: Female Brain Psychology during Various Times

Leading neuro-science psychologists who study the female brain will quickly blame "neurohormone oxytocin" for disparities between mom and mom looking for the brain. Of course, these improvements in the female human brain are necessary to learn further and then use these characteristics to greatness in other issues. Now that I have your attention, for a moment, let's think about it.

It may be helpful to excel in athletics, industry, and policy teams with the understanding that the single woman's brain is different from the couple's, and it would, therefore, make sense to take advantage of it. Both women should consider their minds during these periods and benefit from their abilities. So I wonder, how do we use these processes and the awareness of the different brain chemical agents to increase empathy, trust, and boost communication in order to escape political deadlock?

In the instructional environment, how do we change classroom tasks to enhance memory and understanding of these facts? Does it mean that we should have different ways of educating men and women – particularly women in terms of their (life or relationship cycle)?

How does the female brain cope with drastic changes, such as time, mate ads, marriages, loss of the new (still friendships), mate death, divorce, etc.? Was it time to intervene? Are women taught to combat the drastic shifts from these traumatic times?

Will innovation crack through times of transition? How easy is creativity's demise after a new birth?

Is there even a diet that can be triggered to level the change, or is it bio-hazardous to the offspring and the "locking hypothesis" – are the same brain chemicals able to be used for team bonding during the biological brain transformations or can they rely on other "essential" tasks, assignments or activities? Not "marrying one's work" actually but sort of.

Would a 10-year-old child-bearing woman yes, as in a white mom with eight-to-10 children before the 1920s or a Mormon mom with ten children or a Mexican mom with ten children-do, not the mind switch out absolutely and constantly to life and wouldn't these moms be better empathic team builders, almost to the degree that they can't leap out of that position, even if they want?

Does that make them better leaders in human resources? Perhaps "corporate mothers" business organization to keep the team a family unit as it expands across different industry ships. Would you not like a 10-year-old mom for business relations, a few single women for creative content, and some married women to help to refine this message while selling to baby boomers as you create a Great Public Relations team?

Such facts have so many uses in the real world, right? Or is this far too simplistic targeting a common feature of many in the field of psychology? If we were able to overcome political correctness and talk about these things, we would have gladder and happier people in our culture. We should think about that, and not underneath the tapestry. We need further research if we just encourage people to support themselves. Please take all this into account.

Relationship and Love

Will you, at first sight, believe in love? Okay, a lot of people do that. We think they have found the perfect one and only propose a bitter divorce for their union in no time. These days this scene is not uncommon. All have a lot to learn from these stories.

Loving is not a challenge. Loving is not a challenge. You can't love deliberately or make anyone else fall in love. If you feel attracted to a guy, just wait for a while to find out whether it's love or just another excitement. Time fades away, but real love becomes even more significant.

When you know that you are really in love with someone, you can only move on to friendship. Note, building a relationship takes years while it only takes a moment to break. And you will only be affected by a broken relationship for the rest of your life.

The essential advice on life and friendship would be to get to know your loved one as much as you can. The better you know, the better you feel. Find areas of shared interest and think about discrepancies. Please be kind and affectionate. Other nights head out for dinner and go on holiday together. Such things will keep you engaged and occupied. Always be grateful to your spouse and give unique gifts. Let your particular individual realize how important it is in your life.

Although you do your best, small misunderstandings in a love relationship are unavoidable. It is the secret to the longevity of every partnership. Perhaps these tiny problems inevitably create a significant gap in the long turn between you, and it is almost impossible to meet again.

Another valuable love and relationship advice would be to be very mindful of what your words and deeds could speak to your beloved one. If your friend is irritated by some habit, so try to change the particular behavior. For example, if your wife wants you to quit cigarettes while she is pregnant, then compel her to do that as she is 100% right. Your companion never lies in the same way. Two more lies are expected to cover one. Talk regularly to your companion and show your love.

So the consistency of devotion, truthfulness, and commitment ensures a living and fresh friendship. Your relationship depends heavily on your actions and expressions. Hope this little piece of love and relationship advice will be enough to tell you how to convey your love to your beloved one and how to sustain a long period of close connections with your beloved one.

Relationships usually tend to be content, friendly, and pleasant, and the feeling of 'new partnership' is not any better.

Will anything be done to save a relationship as a marriage falls apart?

So long as you see signs of disappointment, you continue to panic and might even begin to act irrationally – maybe murmuring to yourself, "God help me save my friendship," which may not actually help the situation.

Yes, it is wonderful that you understand that you have to preserve your friendship, but only if you hang on to the facts or the imagination can you learn.

The Course in Miracles says: "It really is up to you to choose the truth or the delusion, but be mindful that one is to let the other go." And if you still try to consider solutions to salvage a broken relationship, the following suggestions may be of use to you.

Precisely what is the partnership problem? If not fixed, both marriage and marriages can have some issues, but specific problems are worse than others, and they will ruin a friendship.

Also, the minor issues must be addressed at the root as you consider things to salvage a relationship, even though they are small, they will slowly grow up to become the cause of marriage and relationship loss.

"The ego wants to 'fix' the issues, rather than at their root, but where they haven't been created." Talk to your partner about the issue Friendship is a journey between two people and you can't solve all the problems yourself.

Don't just want to solve the issue yourself because you have a problem with your friend, and you will have to think about it. You can then solve the issue and learn how to improve the friendship by resolving any problems you might have. Will you really love each other and your partner?

Love is a potent weapon, and if you really enjoy each other, you will be able to save your relationship with that source. When you should keep these ideas in mind, a failed partnership that has complications will be rescued.

Love is a two-way street, and you both have to feel love and be committed to saving your relationship. Will friendship be rescued if there is always a twinkle of love? Indeed, optimism is, of course, at the top of the list of things to do to save a connection.

In order to salvage a broken relationship, you must realize that all relationships can have challenges, but that some challenges are worse than others, and such problems will ruin a connection when not fixed.

It is essential to resolve all difficulties and work together in order to preserve your friendship and love for your partner. When thinking about problems, you can try to save a relationship and solve issues that so much other love and relationships just do not tackle. Be ready and determined to do what is needed to save the relationship.

Chapter 5: In A Relationship, Why Conflict Resolution Skills Are Important

Relationship elements is a subject of interests by moralists, clinicians, scholars, sociologists, and numerous different fields of concentrate since old occasions. A gathering of, at any rate, two individuals with steady collaboration can be characterized as a relationship.

Two people will never concur with each other 100% of the time. It doesn't make a difference how close they are, or what level of moral understanding they have in their relationship; a few issues will emerge. People depend on conflict resolution skills to keep it feasible.

Communication and conflict resolution skills

Toward the day's end, conflicts are settled through a common understanding. It occurs after a lengthy exchange, a bleeding war, or both. A lot of pacifist optimists accept that the dirty war can be skipped and acculturated society can go straightforwardly to exchanges. Those individuals overlook that viciousness is the specialist were all different experts originate from, and expert and influence are fundamental for any dealings.

An individual with excellent conflict resolution skills realizes that reality. He realizes that harmony is accomplished either through dread of common assured decimation, parity, or triumph. All conflicts of all shapes and sizes work in on a similar model.

It's moved toward two different ways, accomplishing the goals of the gatherings included counterbalanced by the expense of securing. The second is persuading one of the two groups that the goals of the conflict itself are more issues than it's value.

How are relational communication and conflict resolution skills comparative? It's imperative to have the option to get indicates crosswise over hostile gatherings while they are in a negative outlook. The two of them require beguile, a high EQ, and the masterful use of words. It is also essential to get the trust and assurance of the two gatherings while staying goal and impartial as a go between. If you are a piece of the conflict, at that point it's significantly additionally challenging to try to avoid panicking, convey, and get the two gatherings to confide in one another.

Conveying during conflicts is difficult. If individuals understand one another, there wouldn't be a conflict in any case.

You would initially need to decide whether the conflict is a miscommunication, misunderstanding, or a genuine contest.

When the cause is detected, the time has come to break separated the issue and resolve the problem individually. A lot of difficulties are only a manifestation of a more profound hidden issue; it is the same as indications of a disease. Assaulting the sign legitimately, for example, a fever will help alleviate the side effect and solace the patient, but it will return if the source, say a disease, isn't handled simultaneously.

What is conflict resolution aptitude

It is the arrangement of capacities that closures a conflict for the individual with such abilities. It's essential to include "positively" in the definition because whimpering while menaces take your treats, isn't a case of conflict resolution skills, regardless of whether it keeps you from being harmed more than you as of now have. Contemporary reasoning is endeavoring a change in perspective to incorporate "agreeably" in the cutting edge definition. However, those strategies are expensive, even to the victor offering ascend to the term Pyrrhic triumph. An individual with genuine ability in conflict resolution can get an ideal result at the very least cost.

Anybody keen on getting conflict resolution skills ought to understand that personal stakes and gunboat discretion is consistently the name of the game. Everybody included wants to get as much as they can from the other party without being too expensive. Conflict resolution skills, by definition, are pretty much a piece of arrangement skills.

Conflicts emerge when more than one individual is after a similar bit of the pie. Ideally, those individuals would figure out how to share simply like what they were instructed in kindergarten. Shockingly, it is anything but an ideal world. Conflict resolution models incorporate harmony arrangements, exchange understandings, and two individuals shaking hands after a spat.

Conflicts should end somehow either through the triumph of one pugnacious or an agreeable settlement. Conflict resolution expertise is the capacity to arrive at that resolution utilizing the least measure of time and assets.

Conflict resolution skills in marriage

Marriage is one of the most weighty relationships an individual can have during their lifetime. Conflicts in marriage have a dependable effect and influence other notable individuals in your life.

Because of the emotional connection to the issue, it is a lot harder to resist the urge to panic during marriage conflicts rather than business issues.

Conflict resolution skills in marriage are increasingly significant and challenging to execute because it's nearer to home.

Couples quarrel and contend all the time, and as a general rule, the arrangement is to give the spouse with a more grounded character a chance to have their direction.

Overlooking issues is also part of the development and a conflict resolution ability. Allowing things to pass and regard it as no big deal is the fastest method to determine a conflict, especially when it's not worth the issue.

There are delicate issues that issue needs to be talked about. If neither one of the spouses has conflict resolution skills to settle the matter, consider contracting a nonpartisan outsider expert, for example, an instructor or specialist. Note that when two people, especially wedded people with kids, contend emotionally, there is an opportunity to exacerbate the situation.

A few people uncover old injuries, resort to insults, ridiculing, and different approaches to criticize their spouse that regardless of whether half-implied could further crumble the circumstance, and add more fuel to the flame.

Conflict resolution skills require a blend of hard and delicate crafts. Basic reasoning and rationale are essential to break separated the issue and find significant and handy answers for unraveling the fundamental sources. Subtle skills, for example, the capacity to assume liability, analysis, and adaptability are also essential to get things going along to an amicable arrangement.

Fixing up issues in your relationship is a piece of life. Develop long haul couples experience harsh occasions only like lethal relationships. However, couples in healthy relationships identify their issues and work together to determine them. It is an endless cycle as problems emerge, and couples hone their conflict resolution skills as they become more established and experience more hardship in their association.

Conflict Resolution Skills for Healthy Relationships

Conflict is an anticipated piece of virtually all relationships. It can also be a significant wellspring of stress. Therefore, with most conflicts, it's essential to discover a resolution. This appears to be an announcement of the self-evident, but numerous individuals smother their indignation or simply 'come to get along.' They imagine that by tending to a conflict, they are making one, and mostly stay silent when vexed. Tragically, this is certifiably not a whole long haul procedure.

Uncertain conflict can prompt disdain and other doubtful strife in the relationship. Significantly increasingly significant, continuous conflict can actually negatively affect your health and life span.

Lamentably, settling conflict can be precarious as well. Handled inappropriately, endeavors at conflict resolution can actually exacerbate the conflict. For instance, specialist John Gottman and his partners considered the manner in which couples battle, and can actually foresee which couples will proceed to separate by watching their conflict resolution skills—or deficiency in that department. (Insight: If you're continually condemning your accomplice's character, or closing down during contentions as opposed to working through conflict in a proactive, aware manner, keep an eye out.)

For the individuals who weren't naturally introduced to a family where immaculate conflict resolution skills were displayed once a day (and—let's be honest—what number of us were?), here are a few rules to make conflict resolution increasingly essential and less upsetting.

Sharpen Your Listening Skills

When it comes to powerful conflict resolution, how adequately we listen is in any event as significant as how viably we convey what needs be. It's indispensable to understand the other individual's point of view, instead of merely our very own if we are to go to a resolution. Actually, only helping the different individual feel heard and understood can once in a while go far toward the decision of a conflict. Great listening also causes you to have the option to overcome any issues between you two, understand where the distinction lies, and so forth.

Shockingly, undivided attention is an aptitude that not everybody knows, and it's regular for individuals to believe they're tuning in, while in their minds they're actually figuring their next reaction, contemplating internally how wrong the other individual is, or doing things other than attempting to understand the other individual's viewpoint. It's also essential to be so guarded and settled in your very own view that you literally can't hear the other individual's perspective.

Connect With Your Feelings

A significant part of conflict resolution includes just you—knowing how you feel and why you feel that way. It might appear that your emotions should as of now be clear to you, but this isn't generally the case. Once in a while, you feel irate or angry, but don't have a clue why. Different occasions, you think that the other individual isn't doing what they 'should,' but you aren't mindful of precisely what you want from them, or if it's even reasonable.

Journaling can be a successful method to connect with your very own sentiments, musings, and desires, so you are better ready to convey them to the next individual. In some cases this procedure raises some truly substantial issues, and psychotherapy can be useful.

Try not to Blame Your Partner

Putting the fault on somebody for an issue that the two individuals are encountering never prompts a reasonable arrangement. Instead, the one assuming the accuse will feel assaulted, constraining them to react to the fault, instead of the issue at hand. A situation that clarifies this pitfall is when an accomplice says, "You're insane for imagining that!" Immediately, the fault is shifted away from the issue, which could be the dread of being undermined, and now the other accomplice will go on edge: "I'm insane? You're the person who's insane!" Note that the first issue has now turned out to be optional to the fault. To stay away from this example, it's smarter to react with "I feel" explanations that keep the central matter at the focal point of the discourse. By saying, "I feel that you're insane to imagine that I would undermine you," expels the fault from the accomplice, while keeping the core of the contention flawless. This methodology will prompt superior communication that praises the sentiments of each accomplice without putting them down.

Look for a Solution

When you understand the other individual's point of view, and they understand yours, it's an excellent opportunity to discover a resolution to the conflict—an answer you both can live with. At times a basic and clear answer comes up once the two gatherings understand the other individual's point of view. In cases where the conflict was based on a misunderstanding or an absence of knowledge to the next's perspective, a straightforward conciliatory sentiment can do some amazing things, and open discourse can unite individuals.

Different occasions, there is somewhat more work required. In cases where there's a conflict about an issue, and the two individuals don't concur, you have a couple of alternatives: Sometimes you can settle on a truce, different occasions you can discover a trade-off or center ground, and in various cases the individual who feels all the more emphatically about an issue may get their way, with the understanding that they will yield whenever. The significant thing is to go to a position of knowledge and attempt to work things out such that is aware of all included.

Realize When It's Not Working

Because of the toll that continuous conflict can correct from an individual, in some cases, it's prudent to place some separation in the relationship or cut ties totally.

In cases of abuse, basic conflict resolution strategies can just take you up until now, and individual security needs to take need. When managing difficult relatives, then again, including a couple of limits and tolerating the other individual's impediments in the relationship can bring some harmony. In friendships that are unsupportive or described by progressing conflict, giving up might be an extraordinary wellspring of stress alleviation. No one but you can choose if a relationship can be improved, or ought to be given up.

Stick to One Argument at once

Notwithstanding expelling fault, it's essential to keep up each contention in turn. Shockingly, when couples battle, it's easy to begin lumping together different issues into one massive victory. When this occurs, the capacity to tackle one problem becomes mixed up in the mix of attempting to take care of the numerous issues, which thusly causes a contention to go nowhere. Couples who can adhere to one dispute have a much improved shot of discovering one arrangement. This methodology allows for disposition of tolerance and understanding, giving each accomplice an opportunity to process their emotions and think of the correct answers together before moving onto to something different.

Practice Assertive Communication

Imparting your sentiments and needs plainly is also a significant aspect of conflict resolution. As you most likely know, saying an inappropriate thing can be like tossing fuel on a flame and aggravate a conflict. The significant thing to recall is to state what's on your mind in a manner that is clear and assertive, without being forceful or putting the other individual on edge.

One successful conflict resolution technique is to place things regarding how you feel as opposed to what you think the other individual is fouling up, utilizing 'I feel' proclamations.

Straightforwardly Express Your Problems

Couples who are having issues may fall back on conduct that stays away from the topic itself. For instance, an accomplice who acts discouraged or dismal may use that as an articulation, rather than legitimately expressing their worry. Something very similar applies to an accomplice who fights back with displeasure or disturbance; their reaction avoids the issue at hand, making more disarray for the two gatherings. So as to discover a resolution, couples should legitimately express what's irritating them in a firm and genuine issue. When the item is out in the open, a good game plan can be instituted.

Communication is Key

It might sound extremely repetitive, but healthy communication between accomplices is the bedrock of any successful relationship. Inside this thought lies an umbrella of tuning in and reaction skills that give direction to couples when contentions begin to follow, or differences start to surface. For instance, one should really focus on the issues or emotions that their accomplice is sharing. This type of listening can be caught up with inquiries or individual identifiers to ensure that one understands what is being said. If an accomplice is laid back in their correspondence or distracted with different issues, the overall communication will never form into something gainful. Utilizing a type of undivided attention and discernment checks will dispose of misunderstandings and give a trustworthy establishment to alleviating future conflicts.

Be Open-Minded

Finally, couples who can stay liberal all through their issues are bound to discover peaceful resolutions that serve the interests of the two gatherings. Getting made up for lost time with one side of the contention doesn't allow for any adaptability with understanding different's worries, so as conflict develops, the chances of gathering in the center are profoundly decreased. To battle this brokenness, accomplices must figure out how to justify a contention from a goal standpoint. They should expel their inner self and think about the two sides of the coin without bias or individual addition. Working inside this mode will allow for reasonable discourse, as well as having the receptiveness to acknowledge the other accomplice's standpoint. When couples can be liberal and goal, they are appropriate to handle an assortment of issues.

Chapter 6: Issues Of Sex And Affection

Issues concerning sexual intimacy are just the tip of the iceberg when it comes to healthy relationships. In other words, they are typically indications of a broader-rooted emotional disorder under the surface. Actually, even the most common physical relationship issues can be traced back to previous interactions and/or concerns that need to be addressed — just ask the therapists who have experienced all of this.

Physical and emotional problems frequently go hand in hand, from less snuggling, touching, and kissing to less frequent (or inexistent) sex. And of course, barring medical conditions, the prevalence of physical contact is also related to the relationship's wellbeing. "I also see a symbiotic relationship between enjoyment, emotional intimacy, and the fulfilment of relationships, each one of these interacts with the other to affect our appetite and excitement.

The growing couple is special, and some people are keener on physical contact than others. But if you start feeling a widening distance between you and your partner.

Questions for Couple

· What if we are not very comfortable talking about our sex life in sessions?

· How often do you want sex?

· How do we improve our sex life?

· How can we be more aware of areas where our habits are incompatible?

· Are you happy with my self-care and hygiene?

· What sexual desires can we enjoy with each other?

Common Issues Related to Sex and Affection

Dissimilar Libido

This is when one partner is more willing to want sex than the other, and it's particularly normal. It can lead to anything, from slight frustration to deep anger and hatred feelings.

Lack of Communication

Sex is such a massive part of a relationship, yet it's probably the thing you talk about the least. The result? Neither of you gets what you want in bed. The fact is, the more we talk about sex, the better sex we'll have.

Boring Sex

You have to shake things up, or else you might fall into a sex rut. This applies to sex, too. It's tempting to blame our partner when sex becomes routine.

When you do not take responsibility and initiate a change, something as small as a different room, a new position, and your partner maybe get bored, and that affects your physical relationship.

No Time for Sex

Between work, kids, family obligations, and just some me-time where you don't want your partner around, it can be extremely hard to make time for intimacy. Whether you've got kids, stressful careers, or both, it's super easy to blame a lack of sex on a busy schedule.

Our Emotional Connection Is Lacking

Although it's Cool if both persons are in it only for the physical release, if you want an intimate relationship but don't feel it, things become more brackish. That is also called as "empty sex," which doesn't sound particularly attractive. To help banish the feeling, work outside of the bedroom to encourage intimacy. "Spend more time together, find new, popular experiences that can help you build a connection, and discuss in other ways what brings joy to you and to your partner.

Starting a Family Has Completely Secured Our Sex Life

Although the lack of sleep and stress can offer real battering to your sex drive, it's not all lost. There are many couples who have been able to resume a fulfilling romantic life after starting a family. Figure out whether logistics prevent you from feeling satisfied or whether the issue is even physical. This might have more to do with unexpressed or unmet needs for emotional connection and intimacy.

Some Couples Just Don't Have Enough Sex or Regular Sex Life

Once the honeymoon period has off this one also forces its way into relationships. The person who wants more sex may feel deprived, but without a discussion, their partner may not realize it. Fortunately, compromises will save the day. "Discuss how much you'd like to be sexually involved, then hammer out a schedule in the middle ground, or set a date you've already decided to be active and have a regular list of things you'd like to do, which could be an issue as well.

Loss Of or Lack of Physical Intimacy

More often than not, the loss or lack of physical intimacy begins in the head. Physical or emotional isolation is often a coping mechanism which evolved years earlier. The problem is, it can fester distrust and exacerbate the divide in the relationship.

There is also an explanation of why withdrawal by men and women will vary, so it's necessary to consider both sides of the coin. For an individual, the physical is generally connected directly for his ego, and when this aspect of a relationship is in trouble, the emotional bond inside the relationship starts to diminish. While women, on the other hand, seek the emotional connection more often, and they will physically withdraw without it. In general, a woman must first wind out of the bedroom, speak and communicate emotionally.

Different Sexual Styles & Lack of Communication

Love is blind, and to bring something different to the table (or bed) for each partner is important. But such differences may also result in a lack of interactions among the couples. Some of the most common problems include starting couples not being on the same side. These can involve libido variations, impulses, dreams, and challenges of excitement. "Still, people find it difficult to express their desires and have open dialogues about enjoyment and sexual contact.

Infidelity

Needless to say, nothing can break a friendship like an indiscretion. They are acting with couples, with over three decades of experience.

Men are much visual and rate their sex life as an enormous way to connect with their partners. When that's absent or rare in a relationship, issues of desire, competence, and interest arise. These issues can take a man to 'test' his level of attraction with other women, whether at work or as stupid as somewhere like a grocery store or a local shop."

On the flip side, when people are looking for sexual pleasure, they are more likely to lie. Emotional phenomenon and the number of married women with affairs are on the increase because they are seeking this validation, not just in the bedroom.

Solution to the Issues

Following are some principles to overcome them:

Reveal

Recognize immediately that what doesn't work. You can't cure or alter what you don't first disclose to yourself. Make sure that your frustration and unsolved issues create roots when they are not resolved. It can begin about something as small as a damaged feeling and then flourish in protective behavior.

Rewrite

Clearly, you cannot recreate your past, but you can erase that from your present life. The rewriting is done by forgiving. Simple terms, a relationship cannot be safe or romantic if the vast majority of us who are non-perfect people are not dearly forgiven. Unresolved conflicts will wreck your relationships without forgiveness.

Renew

Each person must make a nice new day every day to keep a dynamic and colorful relationship, even with the butterflies of a new romance. Renewing means making it better today than yesterday. Even in the face of difficulties, love for one another will flourish, and it should never be taken for granted.

Enjoying a Satisfying Sex Life

Sex, the word can trigger an emotional constellation. The responses are as diverse as the sexual encounters themselves, from passion, excitement, and sweetness to longing, fear, and disappointment. Moreover, in the process of a sex life covering many decades, several men will feel all these feelings, among several others.

Talking To Your Partner

Only under the best of conditions, many couples find it hard to talk about sex. If sexual issues arise, feelings of pain, embarrassment, remorse and anger will altogether impede conversation. Since effective communication is a pillar of a loving relationship, setting up a conversation is not only the first step towards a good sex life but also towards a stronger emotional connection.

Find the Right Time to Talk

Sexual conversations are of two forms. The ones you've got in your bed, and then you've got elsewhere. Telling your spouse what feels good in the middle of lovemaking is perfectly normal, but it's fine to wait until you're in a more relaxed environment to address bigger things, such as clashing sexual desire or orgasm troubles.

Be Honest

You may think that by faking an orgasm, you protect your partner's feelings, but in fact, you start a slippery slope down. The difficulty level keeps increasing as hard as it is to talk for any sexual problem until the subject is hidden under years of failure, hurt and anger.

Maintain Physical Affection

Even if you're tired, stressed or upset about the issues, it's important to engage in kissing and cuddling to establish a physical and emotional connection.

Try To Relax

Before having sex do something relaxing together like, such as playing the game or going outside for a nice meal. Or try calming methods like deep breathing or yoga exercises to relax yourself.

Don't Give Up

If neither of your strategies seems to succeed, don't give up hope. Sometimes, the doctor can assess the cause of the sexual issue and can find successful therapies. He or she may also contact a therapist who can support you discuss problems that might stand in the way of satisfying sex life.

Maintaining a Good Health

Your overall mental, physical, and emotional health tend to be associated with your sexual well-being. So the same healthy habits that you actually keep your body healthy can also shape your sex life.

Don't Smoke

Smoking relates directly to peripheral vascular disease that affects the penis, clitoris, and vaginal tissue blood flow. Additionally, women who smoke continue to go into menopause two years faster than their counterparts who are nonsmoking.

Use of Alcohol in Moderation

Some people with prostate problems believe that one drink can help them relax, but heavy alcohol use can make things complicated. Alcohol can weaken the central nervous system and suppress sexual reflexes. Drinking large amounts over a long period of time will cause liver damage, leading to an increase in man-made estrogen production. Alcohol can cause hot flashes in women and can interrupt sleep, compounding issues that are already present in menopause.

Make Healthy Eating Habits

Every day what you eat affects your health and how you feel right now and in the future. A proper diet plays an essential role in helping you lead a healthy lifestyle. In combination with physical activity, your diet can help you achieve and maintain a healthy weight, lower

Your risk of chronic illnesses like diabetes or heart disease, and encourage overall health and well-being.

It doesn't have to be tough to create and maintain healthy eating habits. You can make a significant impact on your eating pattern and create lasting, healthy eating habits if you start by integrating small changes into your daily activities. Try adding at least six of the next eight goals to your diet each week by adding one new goal.

Make Half Your Plate Fruits and Vegetables

Choose for your meals red, orange, and dark-green vegetables as well as other herbs. Add fruit as part of main or side dishes or dessert to meals. The more colorful your plate is, the more likely you are to get your body's healthy vitamins, minerals, and fiber.

Switch to Fat-Free or Low-Fat

Both have the same amount of calcium as whole milk and other essential nutrients but fewer calories and less saturated fat.

Choose a Variety of Lean Protein Foods

Protein food group includes not only meat, poultry, and fish, but also dry beans or peas, eggs, nuts, and seeds. Select leaner ground beef cuts (where the label says lean or higher by 90 percent).

Compare Sodium in Foods

Use the label Nutrition Facts to select lower versions of foods such as soup, bread, and frozen foods. Select canned foods that are labelled "low sodium," "reduced sodium," or "no added salt."

Drink Water Instead Of Sugary Drinks

To reduce excess calories, drink water from the sugary drinks.

Eat Some Seafood

Seafood has protein, minerals, and omega-3 (heart-healthy fat) fatty acids. Adults should try to eat a variety of seafood at least eight ounces a week. Children can eat minor quantities of seafood. Seafood includes fish like salmon, tuna, and trout, as well as shellfish such as crab, mussels, and oysters.

Chapter 7: Try These New Tools...Won't Regret It

It is well known that love goes through the stomach! Every relationship triggers a hunger that is of a very special kind. How this "thirst" is satisfied is of course best known to the person who is in this very relationship.

But it is not always about the hunger for love and the great lust for the partner, even if it is just at the beginning the only nourishment that lovers need.

Time together through food and drink

Because one thing is quite clear: Nobody can live without the normal and daily nutrition. Where would then be the energy you need to concentrate fully on your relationship and give everything?

Eating is a wonderful way to spend time with your partner. Since time immemorial, nutrition has been the link between people. Nobody wants to be alone and eat their food lonely at the table. Everyone longs for someone to keep them company, especially when a relationship is being lived. Problems of the day can be discussed, be they of a private nature or work-related. Maybe you will find the solution you have been looking for all day. During a meal together, your partner also has the opportunity to think more carefully about worries and to give you a tip that will give you courage again.

But also, the glass of wine in the evening hours is wonderfully suitable to get even closer together. If you do not want to drink it directly after dinner, you can combine it with a nice evening in front of the TV. Cuddle up with your partner and feel exactly the closeness you both were looking for after a hard day.

This way you have something to look forward to in the morning, even if the day still holds so many challenges for you. Look forward to the evening hours and look forward to a cozy meal within your own four walls, or a glass of wine on the sofa: because nutrition connects!

Cooking for the power of love
But of course, it doesn't necessarily have to happen in such a way that you sit down at the table and everything is already prepared, even if it is perhaps your partner's way of spoiling you in this way. It looks the same upside down!
Why don't you cook together and start at the very beginning? This may even include thinking in the morning about what will be cooked in the evening. Juggle ideas and find out what you both really feel like doing after a long day. You might even come up with a dish that hasn't been around for a long time, or something you've discovered completely new! Let your imagination run wild. Once you have made a choice with your partner, you can even go shopping together. Write a shopping list, change the recipe to your heart's content and laugh together. Be curious to see how the end product tastes and looks.

If the shopping is taken care of, it is of course the cooking's turn. Here you can of course not only talk about the cooking itself, but also about completely different things, similar to eating together. However, the advantage of this second option is that you can spend much more time with your love (assuming your everyday life allows it, but this is a decision you can best make yourself).

In this way you will also discover how much fun cooking can be. Maybe you don't like standing at the stove and prefer a quick snack because you are on the road a lot. Or maybe you leave the food supply in the hands of your partner: change this and use your time together in a completely different way. Cook a healthy and tasty meal for both of you that simply makes you want more.

You may even discover a hidden joy in cooking and you may be able to change something in your relationship by taking your place in the kitchen with your partner from now on.

No matter what thoughts the cooking brings to your mind, it brings you and your love even closer together, your love literally goes through your stomach and you may even discover new interests for your future as a couple.

One evening, in a different place

But it is not only life in one's own four walls and eating at the table in the living room that brings life closer together. If this already causes butterflies and big feelings, what about an evening in your favorite restaurant? There are delicacies here that you might never be able to prepare at home. True culinary delights will await you and take you into a completely different world: a world full of delights and culinary fulfillment that you can only rarely experience. Because it is not for nothing that the selected restaurant is your regular restaurant. Also, here the great togetherness and joy begins much earlier.

How about surprising your partner and just telling him that you have something planned for the weekend or evening? Of course, you know only too well that you have chosen the right place.

Make sure that you will have great pleasure and surprise when you park your car in the well-known square. You can be sure that your great love will already be looking forward to the delicious food and a good wine. Who knows, maybe you have chosen the restaurant because it is famous for a very special delicacy.

Just let your soul dangle and enjoy a wonderful evening for two. Because even if cooking together at home has many advantages as well, such an evening arrangement can also shine with many benefits, as you already know. You both need only sit down at a beautifully laid table and make your choice by candlelight. And who knows what else the evening will bring! Not seldom the question of all questions has been asked in the candlelight of your favorite restaurant!

Life is full of surprises and beautiful moments together.

The new diet: together for success

Your partner no longer feels comfortable in his skin and more than once he has tried to start a diet. There is no question that you love him as he is. And this is exactly why you want to see the person at your side happy and content.

So, if it is not an exaggerated ideal of beauty that your partner is pursuing, then support him. Almost any diet makes this possible in principle and shared suffering is, after all, half suffering. Because it is certainly not always easy to do without the delicious things that would otherwise be part of daily life! No more cake in the afternoon and no more pizza at the weekend, no matter how much your appetite calls for it (of course it always depends on the diet itself).

In such a case, encourage your partner and tell him: "Honey, look, I have to do without too! We can do it: together!"

Isn't that a nice thought? You will notice how quickly the loving smile is on your side and how they grow even closer together through the same renunciation. But try not to skip meals altogether. Not only because it is not always good for the body itself, but also because precious time can be lost together in this way.

Sit down together and work out a new diet plan. It does not matter what exactly these new eating habits look like. Perhaps you will only remove a few products from your plan, or from now on you will completely give up meat or industrially produced sugar. Even if your partner's new idea may seem absurd to you, try it and be on his side.

Everyone needs a good body feeling. If this is not available, it can quickly have unpleasant consequences for every relationship. However, it is also important to be on the same level as your daily diet. Because only those who are full and satisfied can also feel happiness and joy and of course pass this on. Give your partner support and convey courage when he or she

pounds not tumbling, or there seems to be a standstill. Always encourage you to keep going and not give up. The goal is within your grasp and you will achieve it together. At some point, you will look back on a time that may not have been easy, but which stands for the fulfilment of a whole new life. Together you will master the hurdles of culinary renunciation!

Staying healthy together

You hear it again and again: How often couples are separated by fate because the loving partner has suddenly fallen ill. Sometimes it is simply life that has sadly "thwarted" a relationship. But it is not always pure coincidence. Sometimes an unhealthy lifestyle can also lead to illnesses that do not immediately tear a love apart, but which can lead to strong impairments. Overweight and diabetes, for example, can be consequences of an incorrect diet. Often too many fats are to blame, but a high consumption of sugar can also harm everyone over time, even if they were otherwise always perfectly healthy.

Do not allow this break in your partnership and taste of a life that still holds so many surprises. Think of the many ventures that you still want to share with each other.

Perhaps you enjoy hiking or traveling a lot! However, this can only work out for both sides with pleasure, if your partner is healthy and stays healthy for a long time.

So, take the time and take a close look at your lifestyle. Are there things you can improve, together with your partner of course? Don't be afraid and talk openly about your thoughts. After all, it's about a life together that will last for many years to come! Here, too, it is important to keep on giving courage and even on bad days to look at what lies ahead of you both. Think of the many wonderful hours that still await you both and set yourself a clear goal: Grow old together!

Perhaps at some point with age comes the time when it no longer matters so much what you and your partner eat. But in those moments, you can reach out your hand, feast to your heart's content and say to yourself: "We did everything just right! Because growing old together is the most important thing in any relationship." *A short conclusion*

Food connects people and that in all situations in life. In the ups and downs of every partnership, nutrition is of great importance. Sometimes, however, this consumption of food is unfortunately forgotten because problems gain the upper hand. But even these problems are eventually resolved and then a good meal triggers great feeling of happiness in the stomach area again.

Time spent together is important and even if everyday life is structured so tightly, food must not be forgotten. Combine the useful with the pleasant and swing the cooking spoon together today. In this way you can select ingredients in a more thoughtful way, live healthier and have lots of fun and pleasure: because you can be together with your partner.

Do not be afraid of the time that has passed, even if eating quietly means going to bed later and therefore getting less sleep. You will soon notice how positive a good and balanced diet can have on your body! You will experience a completely new quality of life and this already in the

first seconds after getting up! Hard to believe?
Then try it out right now! You'll be surprised what happens. Every day can be very special and, in the morning, you will still be able to rave about the delicious food of the previous evening. It doesn't matter whether it is as part of a diet or another change of diet. Enjoy life and love to the full. Give your body gets what it needs to stay fit and vital: a lifetime. Stay healthy and share this positive quality with your partner! Because you want to taste happiness together and should not waste a drop of it!
In this sense: To life and good appetite!

Chapter 8: Attachment Theory

Basics

Knowing both the attachment styles of yourself and your partner can be of incomparable benefit to your relationship. Being able to anticipate both parties' behavior within a relationship – and the possible obstacles you will face can help smooth the path to a healthier, long-lasting connection.

Let's Take a Glance at what to Get When People with each Attachment Type Form a Couple:

Secure + secure

While secure couples in relationships have problems just like everybody else, their relationship is often characterized by excellent communication and empathy. They resolve conflicts more easily and know that they can rely on each other, in good times and bad.

The secure + secure coupling is the most common type of relationship, owing to many people in the population with secure attachment styles, and secures' abilities to cultivate healthy, long-lasting relationships.

Anxious preoccupied + secure

In this relationship combination, the anxious preoccupied partner is likely to test the secure partner's patience by seeking regular assurance. If the secure partner does not act quickly, the edgy, obsessed partner can become anxious and stressed. Despite their inherent securities, this behavior can test the secure partner's patience and cause them to act distantly or pull away, much as a dismissive-avoidant would.

However, a secure partner can be of great benefit to an anxious preoccupied person. The safe can cultivate their partner's trust in the relationship through patient and constant reassurance.

In such a combination, the secure partner can often feel as though they are responsible for the relationship's upkeep and security. The anxious preoccupied insecurities can become self-centered, causing the secure partner to think that their loved one is not invested in the relationship.

Through gentle reassurance from the secure partner, however, this problem should improve over time.

Dismissive avoidant + secure

When partnered with a dismissive-avoidant, a person will often experience distance and coldness within a relationship. This behavior can cause even the most secure people to feel attachment anxiety, leading them to question their self-worth. Even though the securer's requests for assurance will likely be reasonable, the dismissive-avoidant partner will usually not respond to these requests.

For such a combination to work, the secure partner must be aware of their partner's issues and demonstrate enormous amounts of patience to cultivate more security and openness with the relationship.

They are comfortable and confident enough to know someone out there will treat them right in their abilities and self-worth.

Fearful avoidant + secure

This combination has much in common with the dismissive-avoidant + secure pairing. However, the difference is that it is likely to be the fearful-avoidant partner who ends the relationship at the first sign of trouble. This behavior comes about thanks to the fearful, avoiding's fear of being seen for who they are. They are afraid of loss and believe that ending the relationship on their terms will be far less painful than their partner's rejection. They often come to think that this rejection is inevitable, once the fast breaks through the fearful avoiding's façade.

Dismissive avoidant + anxious preoccupied

This potentially damaging combination is one of the most common. The anxious preoccupied will seek the dismissive-avoidant inconsistent attention because of an unconscious need to replay their childhood events. The dismissive-avoidant undervalues their partner, while the anxious distracted overvalues them, leading to a relationship characterized by stress and anxiety.

While the dismissive-avoidant likes to shy away from intimacy and connection, their needy partner will act to confirm the dismissive avoiding's view that all people are clingy. This confirmation makes the dismissive-avoidant more comfortable in the relationship than they would otherwise be, and they often settle into this coupling for the long-haul.

Fearful avoidant + anxious preoccupied

This coupling is among the most negative and damaging. It is also one of the most insecure collars. The anxious preoccupied partner's constant need for attention will scare off the fearful-avoidant partner, who will usually be unwilling to be involved in a relationship in which they are continually fending off intimacy. If the fearful-avoidant partner acquiesces to their partner's need for closeness, it will likely trigger their anxiety. Conversely, if they remain in their comfort zone and keep their distance, the anxious preoccupied partner will respond by increasing their requests for attention.

Anxious preoccupied + anxious preoccupied

This is another coupling that very rarely has a happy ending. The often self-absorbed anxious preoccupied will have trouble anticipating the needs and desires of their partner. With both partners having a deep-seated need for attention and closeness, it is unlikely — although not impossible Do's that they will be able to satisfy each other's desires.

Fearful avoidant + dismissive avoidant

This partnership is an uncommon one, due to both parties being wrong at the positive attachment. Even though both partners may want a less "hands-on" approach to the relationship on the surface, the fearful-avoidant has a deep-seated need for affection that the dismissive-avoidant will rarely fill.

Dismissive avoidant + dismissive avoidant

Unsurprisingly, this coupling is very rare. Cultivating a relationship requires communication — something dismissive-avoidant seek to avoid — a relationship between two people with this attachment style rarely gets off the ground. If they manage to form a relationship, they are prone to ending it at the first hint of conflict, to avoid communicating and resolving it.

Fearful avoidant + fearful avoidant

This is the most uncommon matching, but this is primarily because there is only a small number of fearful avoidant people in the general population. The fearful avoiding's difficulties with communication and self-esteem will make this coupling a challenge. However, it is not necessarily doomed to fail. As both parties have a deep-seated need for intimacy, there is the chance that they can satisfy this need for each other.

Chapter 9: Create Or Re-Create Intimacy -Ways To Charm Your Partner And Get Them To Be Responsive To You And Like You More

Do you get the feeling that your partner doesn't show much interest in you off late? Has the intimacy between the two of you reduced considerably? When people say, all relationships have a shelf life of romance and intimacy after which it starts going downhill; I want to laugh out loud. Of course, things may get boring when you see the person day in and day out, and function on a routine.

However, that shouldn't stop you from continuing the honeymoon. When people say, it isn't working, what they really mean is they aren't working hard enough to make it work. Nothing works on its own – we have to make it work. There are lots of things that you can do to ignite the passion in your married life or add spice to it. Here are a few sizzling tips to recreate or create intimacy in your relationship, get your partner to adore you and get them to be more responsive to your needs and desires.

1. Get Out of the House

Find your passion, and get out of the house to make some time for yourself and your hobbies. It will help your partner value you, even more, when he or she realizes that you have a life and passion of your own. It's necessary to be available at home all the time even if you are a stay at home parent or homemaker!

Find creative activities, join a reading club, volunteer towards charitable causes, sign-up for cooking class, learn a unique form of dancing or martial arts – there's so much to explore. Being a little less available will make your spouse look forward to seeing you or spending time with you, contrary to when you are with each other all the time, and nagging each other. You can also ask your spouse to join you for these activities occasionally. However, the main objective is to have a life of your own, distinct from your time and life a

Build friendships outside the relationship. Exchange notes and stories with friends and enjoy novel experiences to make your time away from your spouse interesting. Time apart is one of the major reasons for the success of any relationship. Owing to the time apart, you cherish your time together. Then there are romantic conversations over the phone. Though your relationship happens to be your primary relationship, it doesn't have to be the only one. Nurture and foster other relationships too to stay off each other's back for a while.

2. Pay Compliments and Don't Forget To Demonstrate Gratitude

During the dating phase, couples praise everything from each other's kerchiefs to 'your cute crooked tooth' to the way your tummy moves when you laugh. However, come long term relationships or marriage, and we believe there's no need to tell the person that we love them or adore certain things about them because they already know or you've already won them over so then there's no challenge in it or fun in the chase. The real chase for keeping a relationship happy and fulfilled in the long term begins once you are married.

One of the most powerful ingredients for a super successful relationship is to pay sincere and meaningful compliments to your partner. Also, avoid taking everything they do for you for granted. Keep an attitude of gratitude if you want to enjoy a rewarding long-term relationship. Appreciate and thank your spouse for little things like packing your lunch, cooking your favorite mean or getting your favorite ice-cream. Appreciate the thoughtfulness behind these small acts.

3. Maintain Passion and Intimacy

Intimacy isn't something that is restricted to the bedroom. Passion and intimacy is a state of mind that can just flow if you both make the right effort. It can be anything from sending naughty texts to your spouse in the middle of a busy workday or leaving little love/passion notes about what you to do to you in the bedroom. Think about aphrodisiacs such as a walk under the stars on a beach holding hands (and ending with a passionate kiss) or a weekend alone in a more secluded place.

Don't limit your passion or intimacy strategies to be defined by what others consider normal or acceptable. You may want to have sex four times a day, and as long as your spouse is alright with it, go for it! Know that over a period of time, priorities in a relationship can change. However, that doesn't make it any less interesting or exciting. Sex isn't the only measure of intimacy. It can also include cuddling over a shared mug of hot chocolate while catching your favorite movie. Intimacy is also conversations, kissing and cuddling.

4. Invest in Your Bond

Isn't it funny how we expect returns everywhere else only after investing and yet largely ignore investing in our relationship while still expecting it to reap rich rewards? Pretty much like everything else in life, you need to invest in your relationship to reignite the spark, make it sexy and enjoy a fulfilling relationship.

I know friends who plan sexy and intimate date nights or go for overnighters while leaving the children with a family member or babysitter. Then there are adult games that can spice up these overnighters for you and your spouse to reconnect intimately with each other, and create memorable moments.

Read a book together, sign up for a relationship retreat, try an online course together and be committed to strengthening your relationship to bring back the spark. You must be committed to the process of bringing back the spark or reconnecting with your spouse before working out a plan to keep working on it periodically. How about a couple of massage or spa treatment once in a while?

5. Be Compassionate

We have a tendency to take advantage of or take for granted the people we love. This is probably because we think we can get away. Take, for example, you have a bad day at work and get yelled at by your boss. Once you get home, you take it out on your spouse because you have no one else to vent it out on, and your spouse will probably tolerate it more than anyone else would.

A healthier way to go about this would be asking yourself if your spouse is really at fault for what happened in the office. Some relationship counselors also recommend asking yourself at the beginning of each day what they can do to make their partner happy. It makes sense to put your best foot forward for the person you love, right?

In a happy bond and relationship, both the partners make an effort to please one another. You may have to sit through long, boring baseball games or watching soppy romantic flicks, talking about virtual gaming strategies and visiting archeological sites when you'd be on a beach. Don't focus on your needs all the time.

6. Don't Leave Any Scope for Misunderstanding

One of the best ways to keep the charm in your relationship alive and get your partner to like you is by eliminating all potential misunderstandings through open communication channels. It is truly astounding how many relationships are destroyed and the spark is killed because both the partners are simply not talking to each other.

Let us consider a scenario for example. Jim and Rose (a married couple) are at the Jim office party to celebrate a huge milestone accomplished by the organization. Jim had a huge role in accomplishing the milestone and is predictably very popular with his managers and co-workers. As soon as Jim and Rose enter the party, Jim is surrounded by a bunch of co-workers congratulating and hailing his efforts.

Since Jim is affable, friendly and congenial by nature, women also find him nice and easy to talk to.

In the entire process, Rose feels ignored and left on her own! She thinks Jim is busy flirting and cracking jokes with his female co-workers while she is left to figure out things on her own. In her mind, Rose feels let down by Jim. In his mind, Jim is relaxed thinking Rose understands everything and is enjoying meeting new people on her. He thinks he is just being nice and friendly while cracking insider office jokes with his female co-workers. Rose doesn't communicate her displeasure to Jim straightaway. Instead, she sulks, keeps mum and reveals her anger through her body language.

Jim doesn't understand why Rose is sulking when she should be having a good time at the party and should be proud of him. Rose, on the other hand, is upset about not being given enough attention by Jim. Thus, there is a mismatch of understanding and how the two partners perceive the same situation. When Jim tries inquiring on their way home what was bothering Rose throughout the party and why she was sulking, she snaps at him for not understanding.

This makes Jim all the more annoyed when in his mind he hasn't done anything wrong at all. He accuses Rose of being insecure, jealous, unreasonable and possessive, which escalates the misunderstanding even further. Wouldn't it have been less complicated if they two had just spoken about each of them felt rather than playing guessing games or expecting the other person to read their mind?

If you really want to ignite the passion or charm in your long-term relationship or marriage, get into the habit of talking to your spouse and telling them exactly how you feel. There will be fewer conflicts, lower unpleasant situations, and much more loving moments once you learn to connect with each other by talking. Get your spouse to like you more by talking about what is bothering you rather than letting the issue simmer over a period of time.

7. Don't Underestimate the Power of Touch

You don't have to jump on each other and have frenzied sex each time you are together. There are small ways through which you can build intimacy by holding hands, hugging your spouse or kissing them on their forehead. How about giving them a relaxed and de-stressing massage?

Physical affection is important when it comes to keeping the spark alive, and it can be revealed through multiple ways than just going on an endless romp session. Even when a relationship is in trouble, these physical gestures of affection can help a relationship pull through. It shows both the partners that they are desired, loved and wanted – something that keeps the relationship alive.

Touch your spouse when they least expect it. For example, wrapping your arms around him or her when he or she is cooking in the kitchen! Or gently massaging their head when they are tired and about to go to bed. These are small gestures that demonstrate your love and care for the other person.

8. Try New Things Together

One of the biggest ingredients of a successful relationship is the novelty factor. Keep the spark in your long-term relationship or marriage alive by doing new and exciting things as a couple. This will help you retain the freshness in your bond rather than letting mundane everyday life take over. Do new, fresh and exciting things together as a couple. It can be anything from skydiving to a backpacking trip in Asia to taking a class together. You may want to learn scuba diving together or play tennis every weekend. I knew a couple who in a bid to add freshness to their marriage or long-term relationship took a cooking class together. And boy did it work!

Pick up anything that offers a break from the usual routine, and gives you both something exciting to bond over. It can be as simple as exploring a genre of film you've never watched before. Adventure activities or sports can get your collective blood pumping, which can lead to a feeling of exhilaration and arousal that can lead to great sex and a bunch of romantic moments. You'll feel more attracted to your partner and driven by the desire to spend more time with them.

Chapter 10: Handling Typical Obstacles

Couples improve in emotion-focused therapy (EFT) by strengthening the protection and reliability in their relationships, allowing them to better listen to and respond to each other's needs. Past experiences of hurt and uncertainty can sometimes prevent people from taking these major initiatives of hearing and reacting.

Your current interactions and experience may well be influenced by your previous pain-coping behaviors. Guilt is a deleterious barrier that may alienate couples and prevent vulnerable experiences from being shared. Relational injuries provide additional barriers to vulnerability. Whenever there is a breakdown of trust or desertion, attachment injuries occur, making it harder to trust your spouse.

You and your spouse might just get along hash out your issues, but you'll still have "valid reasons" for not taking risks or displaying sensitivity in the past. When you've not pushed through the obstacles, they stay. As you attempt to improve your relationship's intimacy, these roadblocks become more apparent.

This section will assist you in identifying roadblocks to attaining greater levels of emotional intimacy with your spouse. You may discover that discussing these roadblocks with your spouse may be the first step in overcoming them in your relationship. Without the assistance of an emotionally oriented therapist who could really help you cope with these difficulties, you might make it increasingly difficult to address these things together.

6.1 Abolishing Shame's Impact

Shame is, at its core, an emotion about one's worth as a person. Guilt, in its most basic form, indicates that your behavior is unacceptable and does not conform to what is expected in your family or community. You may associate shame with humiliation, but it may also mean that you're "inappropriate" in a broader, more deep sense.

If that's the signal you're sending about yourself, it's understandable that you'd want to keep these "bad" ideas, emotions, and feelings hidden. You're terrified of being rejected if people see such things. Loneliness and seclusion are common side effects of attempting to protect oneself from shame.

6.2 Identifying and addressing shame in your own life

Shame can exist in the backdrop of a couple's relationship. Guilt, according to Leslie Greenberg, has a "covering" reaction that prevents transparency and sensitivity to more adaptable core emotions. The link between such a couple's rhythm and the feelings which underpin their seeking and retreating is complicated by shame. Shame hides their deep-seated losses, inequities, and demands. Such requirements are masked by a partner's poor self-perception, which exacerbates the guilt he or she is feeling.

People frequently conceal things they believe are undesirable, including concealing the knowledge that they are concealing them! Shame eventually leads to solitude.

Consider the last occasion you saw somebody who was embarrassed. What clues did you have that he or she was embarrassed? Was it the person's look, anything he or she said, or the way he or she acted that caught your attention? Here are a few examples of shame variables:

- Attempting to avoid direct eye contact
- Managing the situation
- Refusing

- Feeling inadequate or as if you don't belong
- Fear of being labeled as ignorant or inept
- Feeling uneasy and unsure of yourself
- Stepping back
- Curving the head to the side
- Embarrassed
- Observing but not responding
- Being a perfectionist
- I'm starting to feel like an impostor.
- Suffering from a sense of inadequacy
- Having contemptuous or disgusted expressions
- Having a sense of self-consciousness
- Being shy, lonely, or socially distant
- Possessing a sarcastic sense of humor about oneself

When these behavior and attitudes are combined, they can lead to feelings of self-doubt, rejection, estrangement, and inferiority. Those concepts of being undesired, useless, or inferior might be used to arrange how you view yourself.

6.3 Recognizing Shame

People frequently laugh and experience a feeling of unity when they relate to an uncomfortable event. That sense of belonging stems from the reality that everyone has made an unpleasant mistake before. And the laughing they share is a type of affirmation – it shows that others are aware of and tolerates the situation. In the heat of the moment, though, your natural reaction to a humiliating circumstance is to hide it from others. These memories are frequently reinforced by societal demands to fit in along with your social group. Attempts to "save reputation" play a crucial role in social behavior.

Real-Life Problem

Salvador felt self-conscious regarding his look as a kid. He was obese as a teenager and wore used garments which won't match well. He never seemed like he belonged among his buddies. He can clearly remember the insults and jeers he received as a child from people who tormented him. Salvador's professional achievement and social position contrast sharply with his upbringing, although he confesses that his achievement is simply "skin deep." Salvador may appear to be a successful attorney from the outside, but inside he is terrified and never feels like he fits.

Activity

Consider a period when you won't look like you belonged. Perhaps you feel betrayed or ignored. Pose the following questions to yourself:

☐ How made you think about yourself at the time? What term will you use to express how you felt?

☐ Could you think of any occasions when you felt the same way?

☐ What occurs within your body whenever you think about how you feel? What term would you use to describe this sensation?

☐ How much does this sensation occur to you?

☐ What do you usually do when that does come up?

Shame is akin to remorse emotionally. The act of breaching a moral norm, norm, or anticipated action is referred to as guilt. Whenever you break your principles or principles, you may feel guilty, so these emotions may prompt you to take remedial action. You can remedy guilt, but occasionally individuals use self-blame to convert their culpability into shame.

Real-Life Problem

Brad feels that when it comes to Lauren, he rarely pulls things right. He spends a lot of time thinking about her wants and needs. Lauren's happiness is seen by Brad as evidence of his attempts to be a "decent spouse." When Brad believes he is being judged by Lauren, they have their greatest disagreements. Lauren would try to change Brad, and he will become enraged, resenting that she does not recognize how often he is doing for her. Then he turns around and says, "I missed again." I put forth a lot of effort to keep her happy. "I'm a jerk." Lauren is trapped by his loathing for himself. She attempts to tell him what she requires, which he expects, but her expressing incite him to wrath, which he directs either at her or at himself.

Lauren, unfortunately, frequently feels as though there isn't enough room in the relationship for her to communicate her goals and desires. Shame might come from others' harsh judgments or from your own harsh judgments. Knowing the context of your relationship might help you understand the shame cues in your connection. Adverse childhood trauma might make you feel unloved or unaccepted for the rest of your life. Parents can convey "shaming messages" to their children about how they are weak (often aimed at boys), aggressive (mostly aimed at girls), lethargic, unworthy, greedy, or foolish. These rejection signals from infancy become adulthood's refusing thoughts about self.

Shame might give you a sense of control over your abusive behavior. Maintaining a feeling of obligation may give you a sense of authority over circumstances that have broken your beliefs about the world's security and safety.

Perpetrators, who frequently inform the sufferer that he or she is too responsible, could explicitly or implicitly imply these shame and guilt tendencies.

Taming Voice of Shame

Shame might prevent you from feeling other, often painful feelings. Letting pain & brokenness, moving through the brokenness, and ultimately changing the brokenness are all part of the EFT process of dealing with shame.

Change happens when you can accept your brokenness & make room for sentiments that are more adaptable than shame. Self-compassion and a greater awareness of your needs are typically increased when you confront your brokenness in this way.

Having allowed for a person's grief and brokenness is the very first step in using EFT to deal with shame. Shame protects us against unwelcome vulnerability, such as feelings that risk rejection or abandonment. Whenever confronted with these intense core sensations, fear and worry are typical. Moving into this degree of vulnerability necessitates concern and care for such worries.

Letting yourself feel your grief and letting go of your guilt

In the parts that follow, we'll lead you through the steps of addressing your suffering and overcoming the guilt that frequently prevents you from doing so.

Step 1: Confronting your fears in the face of suffering

Embracing feelings of despair and powerlessness as you relinquish control and start to trust your companion and yourself with feelings you've securely handled up until that point is the first stage in this journey. More desperate feelings are frequently present in these experiences, which may be overpowering and encourage both the dread of letting them and the urge to manage them.

Step 2: Identifying Pain Roadblocks

Letting pain exist leads to the exploration of other feelings as well as prior attempts to manage the suffering. Other feelings like grief, rage, and humiliation may arise as a result of opening up about these wounds. You may be upset over previous wrongdoing while also fearing that you don't have the right to be furious. Shame may subdue this brewing rage by telling yourself, "You shouldn't really be furious over that." How could I be enraged whenever I'm partly to blame?"

Step 3: Letting Go of Pain Boundaries

Viewing your suffering more clearly also allows you to recognize how much you've dealt with it and decided to close it out. Once you can notice the shame or diversions which are obstructing your suffering, you'll be able to let go of these restraints and diversions.

Getting rid of shame necessitates a new level of vulnerability. You begin to view yourself and also in a new light without the guilt which has dominated and hidden your sorrow.

Emotional Expression and Loss Grieving

Whenever you face your suffering, you'll be able to recognize the consequences of ignoring it. Communicating these feelings allows you to recognize how you view others and yourself in connection to the suffering more clearly. Being able to be outraged in the face of a violation tells anything about your value and worth: "I'm worth protecting, and I didn't want to be respected this way."

Addressing Yourself

The practice of letting go of your guilt and expressing your grief and anger might help you rediscover your worth and value. You'll be better equipped to stand up for yourself and assume accountability for your interests as you work through your suffering and let go of shame.

6.5 Permitting Your Partner to Enter

Shame, in the end, drives us far from others towards ourselves. Revealing your shattered pieces with your relationship might help you view your relationship and yourself in new ways. There is little need for shame in a stable and sound relationship when your spouse is receptive and available to your painful experiences, and your spouse's empathy may be a source for your self-compassion. Adult attachment research shows the partners in more stable relationships are more going to have a good and deeper understanding of themselves, as well as fewer anxiety and depression issues.

In EFT, a therapist's purpose in dealing with shame is to help clients confront their fear of intimacy and risk sharing, as well as respond to new degrees of vulnerability.

In various ways, shame's "hiding" role makes these interactions more challenging for both parties. Opening out now to your spouse if you're struggling with negative sentiments of self-acceptance involves confronting the inner strife of self-rejection head-on and discovering the power that comes from tackling these internal difficulties together. You no more have to go solo in these hard regions, thanks to your partner's encouraging presence.

It's very unusual for folks who are aware of their partners' fear and fragility to guide talks away from these sensitive areas, which might spark defensiveness and wrath if addressed. You could be afraid to discuss these topics with your spouse for fear of returning to your old conflict patterns and reinforcing the instability of your relation. It's better not to force these talks but to accept your partner's willingness to face shame.

It might be difficult to respond to your partner's sentiments of shame. It's reasonable that you're frustrated, particularly whenever your considerable intentions at respect and compassion are discarded and ignored.

Whenever your spouse is attempting to overcome shame, keep the following suggestions in mind:

☐ Shame is frequently tinged with dread. It's important to remember that when your partner's shame kicks in, he's defenseless and self-protective.

☐ Feelings of anxiety and pessimism are common, so don't be startled. Your spouse is venturing into the unfamiliar ground and confronting feelings that he or she has previously avoided.

☐ Remember that a battle with shame is an internal conflict with oneself. Although your partner's defensiveness may appear personal, it is self-protection when shame is the issue. It's important to remember that this isn't about you.

☐ Show your admiration for your partner's willingness to take chances and the strength it takes to face humiliation. If you know that shame is tough to communicate or discuss, you'll be more likely to provide a safe space for your partner to express his or her vulnerability.

☐ Accepting and acknowledging your partner's struggle are critical foundational elements for safety and security. Meeting your partner where he or she is in the process of letting go of shame allows him or her to move forward.

☐ Validating your partner's experience might help you convey understanding. You don't have to be in your partner's shoes to comprehend what they're going through. Simply seek methods to learn how your spouse has dealt with similar situations in the past and give help in the present.

Real-Life Problem

Will sighed to collect his thoughts. "I understand you assure me I'm not really a failure to you," he continued, looking at Claire. It is difficult for me to believe since that is the lesson I received throughout most of my upbringing. I clung to the thought that I would be able to raise our children differently, but sickness has cast doubt on that and did make me feel less of a man. I know that isn't the case, but I'm concerned you may perceive me in that light. I prefer not to show you that side of myself."

"Will, thank you for informing me." Claire was the one who answered. "I understand that infertility has been difficult for both of us, but I don't consider you a failure or flawed in any way. I adore you because you're my spouse. None of this will make a difference. I understand why you're upset, and I'd like to convince you I'm here to help."

6.6 Overcoming a Breach of Trust

Sue Johnson and her team investigated that certain couples made substantial progress in treatment but did not entirely heal throughout the development of EFT. The couples described a specific episode involving one partner's betrayal or abandonment in a handful of circumstances. Attachment wounds are occurrences in EFT that occur when a partner's prior acts are related to a relationship betrayal experience.

Relational tragedies which impair a couple's continuing connection might manifest as attachment injuries. Attachment damage may become the gold standard for determining whether or not a partner can be trusted and to what extent. Until these attachment traumas are healed, couples are unable to create deeper trust or risk vulnerability. Attachment injuries create roadblocks to trust that must be overcome as a partnership.

Attachment wounds are defined as instances in which the level of trust and dependency in a relationship has shifted. A partner's affair is obviously a violation of trust, but in other circumstances, the importance of the harm is found in the influence the action has had on the wounded partner and what the action symbolizes rather than in the conduct itself (for example, abandonment or rejection).

Activity

Consider an instance when your relationship's trust was tested. How did you deal with it? To analyze the impact of this occurrence on your relationship, consider the following questions:

- Did you and your partner discuss the event? What was the outcome?
- Do you ever bring up the occurrence in your discussions? In your quarrels?
- Do you still have lingering sentiments from that experience? What impact do these sentiments have on your current relationship?
- What efforts did you take following the occurrence to improve your relationship's faith?
- What measures could you take in the area to enhance your relationship's faith?

Since a partner is becoming both the cause of and the cure for emotional anguish, attachment damages are intrinsically difficult to resolve. As a consequence, the connection is intrinsically unstable. As a method of coping with their uneasiness, partners decide not to trust one another again. Some injuries occur without the perpetrator's knowledge. Even though their effects on a couple's level of intimacy, many injuries often go unacknowledged in a relationship.

Couples distinguish two emotional reactions in reaction to these traumas, making it difficult for them to move past, much alone admit, the traumas. The long-term effects of the damage might alter how couples view their relationship.

6.7 Common Factors Shattering Trust

Attachment injuries can happen in a number of ways. A few of these circumstances are more apparent than others. The following are some of the most prevalent scenarios in which attachment injuries occur:

- Unfaithfulness and other interpersonal partnerships are examples of relationship deceptions.
- Absence of a partner at a time of transformation in one's life (for example, the birth of a child, having a child move out of your home, retirement)

- The departure of a companion during a period of bereavement (for example, a miscarriage, the death of a child or family member).
- Absence of a partner throughout a period of transition (for example, medical illness).

6.8 Identifying Barriers for Your Safety

Attachment injuries typically appear after a couple has progressed through therapy. Couples who express less emotional suffering and respond less to one other may be getting along, but they aren't engaging deeper parts of their relationship that they have walled off. These injuries come to life when the emotionally oriented therapist encourages couples to take more emotional risks in trusting one another.

The injury is occasionally openly stated as an ongoing complaint by the wounded partner. Because the offending spouse downplays the severity of the hurt, it does not get resolved. In other circumstances, the offending partner's rejection of the pain prevents the pair from discussing the harm, and the relationship gets along without ever discussing the prior harm. The attachment damage remains latent in both circumstances until the pair is challenged to trust each other in new ways.

Because of damaged spouses, attachment injuries might sometimes go unaddressed. The damaged partner may be resistant to the offending partner's attempts to treat the harm. "I just can't trust that he has truly changed," the damaged partner could say. How do I know he's serious about it? That's simply a bunch of words." Similarly, the hurt partner may be terrified of being vulnerable once more. "I can't let my guard down," he would remark. I'd already let it down once.

It's simply too dangerous." In order for regret and apology to heal, a wounded spouse must believe that his or her spouse cares and is linked to the anguish that the harm created.

6.9 Dealing with Damage Done

The emotionally oriented therapist assists the wounded spouse in examining how the damage has damaged the relationship and their feeling of self-worth.

As time passes, the wounded spouse becomes more aware of his demands at the time of the injury, as well as the harm is done to his faith in his partner. The therapist also assists the offending spouse in accepting and comprehending the damaged spouse's anguish and desire for a safe and trustworthy connection.

When an assaulting partner is affected by these wounds and the unmet demands, he or she expresses sorrow and sorrow. Such confidence & assistance demands are frequently indicators of a partner's devotion to the couple's relationship.

6.10 Regaining the ability to trust

The guilty partner responds to her partner's needs with a concerned and guarded reaction in the later phases of healing attachment damage. When the couple's connection is rebuilt on trust, they can return to good emotional rhythms. Couples who had successful therapy for an affliction reported having more forgiveness towards their spouse.

Chapter 11: Significant Habits Of

Good Relationships

Habits have a significant effect on your relationship. When it comes to having a good relationship, there are certain behaviors that can have a strong and positive impact. It's essential for you to be conciseness when forming routines, especially for your relationship.

Significant Habits of Good Relationships

You need to make an effort every single day to perform them, so they become part of the routine to you.

Always show respect

Showing respect for your partner is a habit worth making, as it is an ingredient necessary to create a happy, safe, and long-lasting relationship. You express your affection, appreciation, and comfort when you show respect for your partner. If you show contempt, you convey that your spouse is not acknowledged. Respecting your partner, despite variations, is all about valuing them for who they are. You may have a other view on life, but that doesn't mean you can neglect and put down your friend.

If experiencing conflicts, make sure you respect the disagreements between your spouses. This does not allow you to offend your partner in front of friends and family or in public. Also, show respect, especially when you're in disagreement. There will be moments when you disagree on a topic, and it's going to be how you approach this problem as a team that's going to make the world difference.

Go for a stroll with your friend

This is a ritual formed by a husband and where they find a deeper connection in their relationship. If you love nature and spend time with your mate, make it a habit to walk— either in the mornings before beginning your day, or at night. For example, husband and wife walk on Sunday mornings and in the evenings. It's a mental decision which they make to go out together every day. It encourages communication, fresh air access, and quality time. Once you develop this routine, the body may actually want to go out. It is noticed this with couples when they made it a habit to walk at night, and on Sunday mornings, their bodies became ready to spend the quality of time. Walking with your partner also promotes good fitness, and can be as easy as walking up and down the block. Decide how long and how often you'd like to walk with your partner; the major thing is to being on the same page and making sure you make the mental decision to build this routine together.

In the night time turn off the television and be with your friend

How can you relate to your partner when there's always television? There is no bond established when you both look at the television screen endlessly in the evenings. Take the mental decision to turn off the television at night, and spend time together in quality. You may be able to snuggle and watch a movie sometimes but avoid watching TV most evenings.

Take the time to chat with your friends about their day and how they're doing. The behavior causes love and attachment. Snuggle up and chat on the sofa with your partner; talk to each other and what you two can do to strengthen your relationship. Whether it's preparing for the next holiday or your next date night, there'll always be something to consider. Focus on developing your relationship and discuss issues you need to tackle.

In the morning, take some tea with your friend. This simple gesture indicates a great deal to my husband. He loves drinking coffee and shows morning love and affection to get it to him. If your partner likes to drink tea in the morning, and through this act of service, create that habit, Express love. When you bring a cup of tea to him, it shows you care, and this is one way you can show love to him. Wake up a few minutes earlier so you can spend some quality time together with your partner before going on the job. This is an easy yet powerful habit of happy relationships.

Share positive attributes about your partner to others

'Habit of sharing positive attributes about your partner can help the relationship deepen. Alternatively, sharing negative attributes about your partner will only build a tall wall between you two. Would you know a couple who always argue with friends in public and show negative characteristics about each other? This is a bad habit that inevitably wrecks a friendship. This destructive behavioral pattern causes distrust, disconnection, and disrespect. Get used to projecting positive attributes for others. An optimistic behavioral trend produces respect, appreciation, and devotion.

Scroll down to read the article Are you reaching your full potential?

Take the life-potential evaluation of Life hack and get a personalized report based on your unique strengths, and find out how to start living your entire life and achieve your full potential.

Reconnect throughout the day

We have such busy routines that it can be the last priority to communicate with your partner throughout the day, but if you want a healthy, long-lasting relationship, reconnecting-connecting-connecting with your partner throughout the day is important. It is as easy as sending a romantic text or calling your partner on the way home during your lunch break. This habitude is meant to keep your partner linked and focused. You can still take the time to send a text message or send your friend a phone call, even if you have a hectic schedule. Render yourself artistic. Think about ways you can reconnect-connected-connect with your partner all day.

Take time to think

Take time to think out how you feel loved most and how your partner feels the most affection by looking at these 5 love languages. Imagine having a tank of love inside of you. Your love tank is filled up each time your partner speaks your love language. Your love tank runs low each time your partner doesn't convey your love language. When it comes to important behaviors of happy relationships, establishing the habit of speaking the love language of your partner on a daily basis creates in your relationship, passion, affection, and warmth.

Cooking and cleaning

The cooking with your partner is always much more fun. I know when John helps me; I enjoy cooking a lot more.

Cooking together builds intimacy, communication, and love; creating and eating food when you are with your partner becomes an intimate act. I express my love by cooking and eating with my husband (with TV off), which creates a deeper bond between us. This is a big opportunity to spend time together in quality.

If you prefer cooking or your partner, make it a habit that the other person cleans. John and I have a habit of cleaning up afterward whenever I cook, and vice versa. It shows appreciation for my cooking when John cleans after I cook and that he values me. It is important that you always love and respect your spouse, even if the cleaning of the dishes is as easy as that. It's nice to know John appreciates the love I put in my cooking, and it's a sign of love-affection to want to do the dishes Become mentally stronger!

Become Stronger

Every day shows love for your partner welcomes to your partner! It is just as simple as this. Whatever love you want to show in your relationship, do it. Do this on a single day. It's about showing your gratitude to your partner when it comes to important traditions of happy relationships. This can be leaving a love note at the end of the day before going to work or taking flowers home. It goes back to the love language of your mate. Find the language of love for your partner and show your gratitude for your partner through their language of love. If your partner feels valued by quality of time, make sure "turn off" and focus your attention on your partner when you get back home from work. Sit down on the couch, and be with your partner. Whichever language your partner loves, make sure you speak the same language. Make it a habit of showing your partner appreciation every single day.

Working together as a team towards objectives (short-and long-term)

A happy relationship focuses on short-and long-term objectives. Unhappy couples have nothing in their lives to look forward to. Focus on creating, establishing, and attaining goals within your relationship. Happy couples have ambitions, small as well as large. Follow this template setting target, and start cultivating your partner link.

Spend quality time

In the morning to show and be with a partner before beginning the day. Surely this practice starts to rob your relationship and the bond you have with your partner. We have such hectic schedules that it is even more important to take the time to talk with your partner in the mornings. Reflect and understand what brought you two together. It's easy to allow tension, anger, and distractions to get in the way of a happy relationship, but when you take the morning time to love and appreciate your partner, you're building a routine that's filled with comfort, affection, and care.

Conclusion

We have finally come to the end of this book, and I hope that somehow, someway, this book helps you and your spouse to find yourselves again. You need to know that this is going to take some time, and some work. It also depends on how bad things have gotten between you and your loved one.

That said, I don't want you to quit. You need to ask yourself if your love is worth fighting for. I assume the fact you're reading this book right now means it really does matter! So you must be willing to put in the work. Set your ego aside and allow a chance for your love to get back to where it was, or even better. It is my sincere hope that you know how much it matters for you to be willing to understand each other as a couple. I hope that even without the exercises in these books, you make it a point to keep checking in with your partner, and the state of your relationship.

I will tell you one thing: Just because it's going to take some work, does not mean it has to be all drudgery. Spending time with your lover checking on your relationship can be very enjoyable! If you allow yourselves, you will notice you're growing closer and closer to one another, day after day. That is definitely well worth it, in my book.

If there is one thing I would like to stress, it is this: Make loving a daily business. You know you can't just skip work whenever you feel like it, for whatever reason — not if you hope to keep having a roof over your head and food to eat. So, in the same way, get serious about your relationship. No one is wired to be alone. This person has chosen to be with you. The least you could do is to be the best version of yourself that you can be, for them. It's always worth it.

I highly recommend that you figure out the best ways to show your partner that they mean a lot to you, every day. Don't just show them you love them the way you're used to showing it. Show them in ways that they can understand. This means getting to know what your love loves to feel and experience, so that they know you really and truly love them. Even in loving, it is possible to be selfish. Don't assume just because you're showing them love in **your** love language, that they know it all the time. Step outside of yourself sometimes, so you can love them the way they truly want and deserve to be loved.

Another thing I need to stress is that there is no such thing as the perfect human being. Beyoncé is a goddess, and she is flawless, but only Jay Z's therapist would know what's really going on with them. What I mean by this is that you should not put undue pressure on your partner for not always being one hundred percent Prince or Princess Charming. Sometimes things happen, they get stressed out, or they forget. In times like these, do lovingly recall all the good that they have done, the good that is still in them. Be there, loving, patient, gently nudging them back to the person they truly are.

If you think you're going to make any headway by whining about the fact that things are no longer the way they used to be between you two in the beginning, then you've got another thing coming. Don't whine. Do something. Be proactive about your relationship and getting it back on track. Your partner might have the same feelings about you, so why don't you take the lead in bringing back the spark? Don't wait. Just act! Your partner will appreciate you and love you for it even more.

Love is not a race. It's a journey. It only ends when death do you part. At least, that's how it should be. That is how it is when two people come from a headspace that says no matter what, I love this person, and we will always get through whatever life brings out way.

When you're in love, truly and selflessly, you come to realize that there is no mountain high enough and no valley low enough, just like the song says. There is nothing two people determined to be together cannot overcome. Know that, and you're more than halfway towards having the relationship most people only ever dream of but never actually experience!

I can tell you from personal experience that deliberately building your relationship is an incredibly satisfying thing to do. There is nothing like moving about your day, actively seeking new ways to put a smile on this special person's face and heart! In fact, my partner and I have made a game of it, and it has caused our love savings account to blossom and overflow beautifully! Several decades later, it still feels like the first day we met every day.

I guess you could say we have cracked the code to making the honeymoon last a lifetime. Takes a lot of work, but it's worth it. I only have one head. Last time I checked, so did my partner — and I checked just a couple of minutes ago. If we could take our relationship to where it is now, then so can you.

I am rooting for you and your spouse or partner one hundred percent. There is no doubt in my mind that you both can be a lot better than you already are, together. Are you willing? Are you open? Then that's all you need. Put in the work, and watch the good times roll with each other. True love is no myth. But it ain't no walk in the park either. Maybe not at first. However, once you build those loving habits, and realize you're both in this for better or worse, then there is absolutely nothing that could get in between you two. Ever.

www.ingramcontent.com/pod-product-compliance
Lightning Source LLC
Chambersburg PA
CBHW071844080526
44589CB00012B/1096